art

An A–Z Guide

Selected & Written by

Shirley Greenway

FRANKLIN WATTS

A Division of Grolier Publishing

Danbury, Connecticut

New York   London   Hong Kong   Sydney

For Felicity,
with thanks...

Cover credits: *Top left:* The British Museum, London. *Below left:* Musee Biot-Fernand Leger (c) RMN-ADAGP
(Photo: (c) RMN - Gerard Biot) *Right:* William Harnett, *Still Life ~ Violin and Music.*
The Metropolitan Museum of Art, Catherine Lorillard Wolfe Fund, 1963. (63.85) Photo; (c) 1991 The Metropolitan
Museum of Art

Produced in association with **ticktock** *publishing ltd*.

Writer and Picture Researcher: *Shirley Greenway*
Editor: *Felicity Trotman*
Managing Editor: *Penny Worms*
Designers: *Graham Rich, Phil Clucus*

For Franklin Watts: Doug Hill

Library of Congress Cataloging-in-Publication Data

Greenway, Shirley.
Art: an A–Z guide / written by Shirley Greenway.
p.cm.
Includes bibliographical references and index.
Summary: A dictionary of terms and concepts related to art history and art techniques,
including artists and schools of art.
ISBN 0-531-11729-4 (lib. bdg.)   0-531-16553-1 (pbk.)
1. Art–Dictionaries, Juvenile.
2. Art—History–Dictionaries, Juvenile.
[1. Art–Dictionaries.] I. Title. II. Series.

N33 .G74 2000
703—dc21
00-024899

Contents

Introduction 5

Abstract Art 6

Action Painting 8

Balance 10

Calligraphy 12

Cartoon 14

Carving 16

Classical Art 18

Collage 20

Color 22

Composition 26

Computer Art 28

Conceptual Art 30

Cubism 32

Dada 34

Decorative Arts 35

Drawing 38

Earth Art 40

Engraving 42

Expressionism 44

Fauvism 46

Foreshortening 48

Fresco 50

Illumination 52

Impressionism 54

Landscape 56

Lithography 58

Masquerade 60

Mobile 62

Mosaic 64

Mural 66

Oil Painting 68

Op Art 72

Pastel 73

Perspective 74

Photography 76

Pointillism 80

Pop Art 81

Portrait 84

Post-Impressionism 86

Pottery 88

Prehistoric Art 91

Proportion 92

Realism 94

Relief 97

Renaissance 98

Romanticism 100

Sculpture 102

Silk Screen 105

Stained Glass 106

Stencil 108

Still Life 110

Street Art 112

Surrealism 114

Symmetry 116

Tapestry 117

Theme 118

Watercolor 120

Weaving 122

Woodcut 124

Acknowledgments 125

Index 126

Introduction

Humans have been communicating through artwork for centuries. When you look at a piece of art, you are looking through the eyes of the artist. You catch a glimpse of the culture and time period in which the artwork was created. Styles in art are often influenced by such things as wars, scientific discoveries, and changing religious beliefs. Though you may appreciate these changing styles, in order to share your observations you need to learn the vocabulary used by those who create, study, discuss, and write about art. In the art world, many familiar words such as "composition" and "cartoon" have different meanings.

By understanding this vocabulary of art, you can discuss various movements in art and describe an artist's style and technique. For example, you will be able to compare the styles of two artists from two different centuries, such as the nineteenth century painter Thomas Eakins (page 95) and the twentieth century painter Pablo Picasso (page 33). Eakins was a realist. He painted the human figure precisely, almost as it might appear in a photograph. Picasso, a cubist, interprets the human figure much differently, using strange and unnatural shapes.

This book features 59 words, which are important to an understanding and discussion of art. As you read and learn these words and how they relate to the illustrations, you will be prepared to make intelligent observations about paintings and other pieces of art.

Martha Richardson
Richardson-Clarke Gallery
Boston, Massachusetts

Abstract Art

Art that does not represent recognizable scenes, objects, or figures—although it may be inspired by them—is called **abstract art.** There are several types of abstract art. CUBISM is a distorted (altered) expression of reality. ACTION PAINTING is the use of line and color to create surface texture. Another type of abstract art is the arrangement of simple geometric shapes and colors in space.

4 X 5 = 20, undated Wassily Kandinsky

Abstract Design

A group of artists and designers came together in Holland in 1917. They called their work de Stijl (Dutch for "The style"). The style they developed was abstract, with geometric shapes and flat, bright colors. It worked best in the DECORATIVE ARTS. Famous examples of de Stijl furniture are like beautifully designed pieces of sculpture.

Red and Blue Chair, 1918
Gerrit Rietveld (1888–1964)

Wassily Kandinsky (1866–1944)

Around 1900 the Russian artist Wassily Kandinsky turned away from figurative images. He wanted to compose paintings like music—to "hear" the "inner sounds" of objects and paint them in "harmonies" of color. His paintings glow with humor and high spirits. He was the first truly abstract painter.

Painting the City

If music inspired Kandinsky and abstract art, then America in the early years of the twentieth century was the place to hear it—loud, brash, and with a jazz tempo. New York was its heart. There traffic moved along long, straight streets, and skyscraper canyons boomed with the sounds of rush hour. The Dutch painter Piet Mondrian (1872–1944), a member of the de Stijl group, moved to New York in 1940. By flattening forms and brightening colors, he made his LANDSCAPE paintings more and more abstract. Over the years he created a unique combination of geometry and color, to represent space— a "shorthand" for an already fast-moving century. When he came to New York, he used this shorthand to catch the city's shape, movement, and music in paintings such as *Broadway Boogie-Woogie.* The seventy-year-old artist took up dancing—and gave the world a lasting image of modern city life.

Broadway Boogie-Woogie, 1942–43 Piet Mondrian

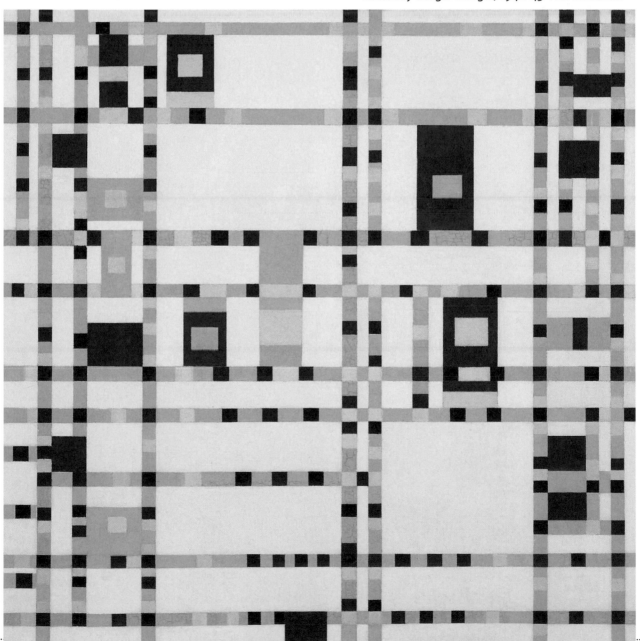

● *See also pages 8–11, 20–21, 28–29, 32–34, 62–63, 72, 81–83, 116*

Action Painting

Action painting was one strand of abstract EXPRESSIONISM, the most important movement in American art from 1940 to 1960. It was a style based on line and movement rather than shapes and COLORS. The physical process of painting was part of its style. Action painting was an art of pure self-expression—the painting "grew" as the artist covered a huge canvas with many layers and textures of paint.

Jackson Pollock (1912–56)

When Jackson Pollock was four years old, he lost part of his index finger in an accident. He could not draw; but he *could* paint! Huge canvases laid on the floor were filled with layers of paint—spattered, dripped, and flung from pots in a frenzy of activity. Pollock worked from all sides at once. He became the most famous artist in America, with a pop-star's fame. Photographers came to record Pollock in action. The paintings have no focal point, or horizon; no "up" or "down." But he meant it when he said, "Don't look for anything. React."

Frieze, 1953–55 Jackson Pollock

Tête Éclatée (The Fragmented Head), 1958 Karel Appel

The Expressionists

In the 1930s events leading up to World War II caused upheaval in Europe. Many artists took refuge in America. New York became the home of a new movement in art—abstract expressionism. It combined the ideas of the European newcomers with those of American painters responding to a changing, dangerous world. Chief among the American painters were the Dutch-born Willem de Kooning (1904–97)— who had arrived in New York as a stowaway in 1926—Franz Kline (1910–62), who worked almost entirely in black and white, and Jackson Pollock. In Europe after the war there was a new interest in EXPRESSIONISM, especially in the work of artists such as the Dutch painter Karel Appel (b. 1921). Appel's paintings had the same vigorous, almost savagely expressive quality and thick, textured surfaces as American action paintings.

● *See also pages 6–7, 12–13, 22–25, 44–47, 68–71*

Balance

When all the parts of a painting or SCULPTURE are combined to produce a pleasing sense of evenness or harmony in the finished work, it can be said to have **balance**. Among the ingredients that create balance are the content of the work and the feelings or atmosphere conveyed by the artist.

Andrea del Sarto (1486–1531)

Andrea del Sarto was the painter *senza errori* (Italian for "without fault") of the High RENAISSANCE in Florence. He painted FRESCOES, altarpieces, and easel paintings with religious THEMES—which he often set in his own time. The warm, rich colors, effortless drawing, and quiet, thoughtful expressions in his paintings create a feeling of serenity and calm. His compositions—as below, in *The Visitation*—have a strong geometric framework. Crossed diagonal lines lead the eye to a triangular shape, made by the two central figures. They lean toward one another, framed by the rectangle of an open doorway. Gray stone steps spread out on either side, giving positions to the other figures. This moment of meeting is held in perfect balance.

The Visitation, 1520–30 Andrea del Sarto

Jan Vermeer (1632–75)

The Dutch painter Jan Vermeer was the president of the Painter's Guild of Delft. He sold the work of other guild members, but none of his own. When he died he left just twenty-nine unsold jewel-like paintings. He wasn't recognized as one of the great masters of the seventeenth century until two centuries later. Vermeer's detailed paintings of Dutch middle-class life show us an ordered and perfect world. These small paintings are brilliantly composed, with crowded foregrounds and very deep PERSPECTIVE. They seem much larger than they are.

A Young Woman Seated at a Virginal,
1670 Jan Vermeer

Smooth Perfection

Vermeer's colors are deep, clear, and unusual: blue, lemon-yellow, gray, black, and white—as Vincent van Gogh noticed in 1874. The paint was thinned and applied smoothly. The surfaces look like "crushed pearls melted together." The colors gleam in light falling gently from the left. Through all of his work, Vermeer left nothing ill-considered or half-finished. All his pictures show his very great care. To some critics his work was cold and mechanical, but to another, Vermeer's "art had only one melody—just like a nightingale or a lark only have their own."

● *See also pages 22–27, 68–71, 74–75, 92–96, 98–99, 116*

Calligraphy

Calligraphy is the art of fine handwriting. It is an ancient Chinese technique, closely linked to painting. In calligraphy, the shape and decorative quality of the lettering is the most important element. European penmanship began in ancient Rome and was used in the medieval art of ILLUMINATION. Chinese calligraphers use brushes for both painting and writing. In the West, brushes, quills, and steel-nibbed pens are used.

The Oriental Masters

The Chinese developed calligraphy during the Shang dynasty (c. 1766–c. 1122 B.C.) as a branch of painting. Instead of letters, the Chinese language is written in ideograms (visual symbols). Chinese calligraphers follow strict rules to shape each symbol. The lines of a poem become small abstract compositions. Chinese, Japanese, and Arabic calligraphers remain the masters of this delicate art.

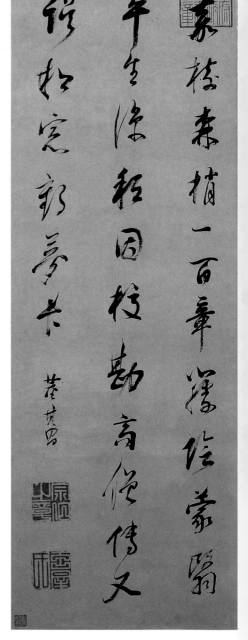

A Four-line Poem in Cursive Script (Cao Shu), Hanging Scroll, Ink on Paper, 17th century
Dong Qichang (1555–1636)

A dam lay ybounden,
Bounden in a bond;
Four thousand winter
Thought he not too long.
And all was for an apple,
An apple that he took,
As clerkës finden written
In their book.
Nor had the apple taken been,
The apple taken been,
Then had never our Lady
A-been heaven's queen.
Blessed be the time
That apple taken was!
Therefore we may singen
Deo gracias!

Fifteenth-century Carol, 1925
Edward Johnston (1874–1944)

The Art of Handwriting

Writing on paper began in Rome with the arrival of Egyptian papyrus paper. The Romans developed cursive (joined) script, later called italic. In monasteries, monks produced decorated manuscripts, with the text lettered in a fine uncial (inch-high rounded) script. These traditions became the basis of modern Western calligraphy. Good calligraphy, like good DRAWING, has accuracy, rhythm, BALANCE, a flowing line, and style.

● *See also pages 8–9, 38–39, 52–53*

Die Schattige, 1939 Paul Klee

Paul Klee (1879–1940)

The Swiss artist Paul Klee produced a vast range of work in many different styles throughout his career. He was curious and imaginative and found inspiration in many art forms—including calligraphy—making them all part of his own unique vision. He used COLOR and line in new and delightful ways. Patterns of dark and light "calligraphic" markings skip across the surface of his paintings.

White Writing

The work of the American painter Mark Toby (1890–1976) was also influenced by calligraphy. He traveled widely, especially in the Far East, and studied Oriental art and thought. He called his personal style "white writing." Toby filled his large canvases with soft COLORS. Over the color he ran layers and layers of calligraphic lines, like written lace—their meaning teasing but well-hidden. His work looked like ACTION PAINTING, but grew out of contemplation, not activity.

Edge of August, 1953
Mark Toby

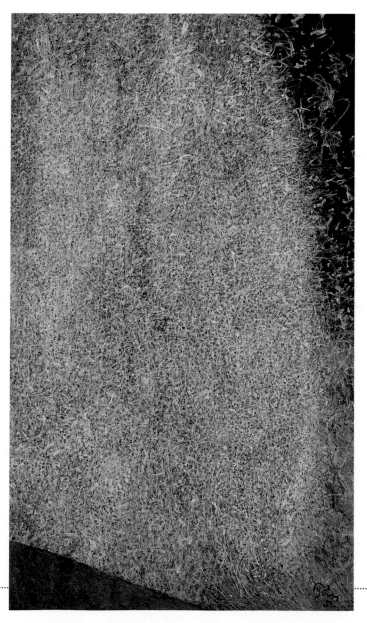

Cartoon

In art, the term **cartoon** has two meanings. It originally referred to a full-size DRAWING that served as a model for a STAINED-GLASS window, TAPESTRY, or wall-painting. It is now used to describe a satirical or humorous drawing that pokes fun at society or politics. Strip versions of cartoons first appeared in newspapers, and became the basis for comic books.

Cartoons as Sketch Designs

Preparatory cartoons for FRESCO paintings were drawn in charcoal line. They were "pricked" onto wet plaster before painting began. The charcoal trickled through the pinholes, leaving a faint outline.

The Virgin and Child with Saint Anne and Saint John The Baptist, c. 1500 Leonardo da Vinci

Artists often made a sketch to scale (full size) for a planned painting. Leonardo da Vinci's drawing of *The Virgin and Child with Saint Anne* is one. The painting itself was never done, and no painting could improve upon this sublime sketch. Cartoons for tapestry were painted in full color as a guide for the weavers. Among the most famous examples are the Raphael cartoons, painted in 1515–17 for huge tapestries in the Sistine Chapel telling the stories of the Apostles. Only ten of the sixteen tapestries were made, but the cartoons now hang in a special gallery in the Victoria & Albert Museum in London.

The Miraculous Draught of Fishes, (cartoon for tapestry), 1515–17 Raphael Sanzio

Satire and Social Comment

The art of visual satire really began in eighteenth-century England. William Hogarth (1697–1764) attacked the wicked behavior of the nobility in hugely popular engravings like *The Rake's Progress* (c. 1735). James Gillray (1757–1815) became famous for his biting satires of political life. His caricatures (exaggerated depictions) of the royal family, the aristocracy, and politicians were bold, witty, and cruel. Thomas Rowlandson (1756–1827), a brilliant draftsman, created unforgettable scenes and characters. They were coarse and earthy, but gentler than Gillray's cartoons, and gorgeously painted. Rowlandson's cartoons showed the English at their most pompous and self-satisfied.

The tradition of serious artists turning their hands to social satire lives on in the work of artists such as Gerald Scarfe (b. 1936) and Ralph Steadman (b. 1936).

Entrance to the Mall, Spring Gardens, 18th century Thomas Rowlandson

Political Playing Cards, 1983 Gerald Scarfe and others

La Promenade en Famille: A Sketch From Life, 1797 James Gillray

● *See also pages 42–43, 50–51, 66–67, 98–99, 106–107, 117*

Carving

Carving is the art of cutting into stone, bone, ivory, or wood to create decorative objects. Carvers use special tools to make different types of cuts and notches. Carvings may be free-standing or in RELIEF (seen from one side only).

Carving a Leaf...

Carvings may be large or small, depending on the size and shape of the original material. Large pieces of furniture are often made from several pieces of wood, each carved and decorated. One of the most popular designs found on furniture from northern Europe is the acanthus leaf, a detail borrowed from classical architecture. It can often be seen as the carved "crown" to a cupboard or chest.

"L'Endimion": Carved Chest in Ebony, French c. 1645

Cravat, Carved in Limewood, c. 1690 Grinling Gibbons

Grinling Gibbons (1648–1721)

Grinling Gibbons was the master of delicate woodcarving. He worked for the English kings Charles II and George I. Gibbons' favorite subjects were fruit, flowers, and leaves dotted with shells and small animals—all in perfect, natural detail. The English writer Horace Walpole said of him, "There was no man before Gibbons who gave to wood the loose and airy lightness of flowers." Walpole surprised his French guests when he appeared wearing this beautiful cravat (neck-scarf) of wooden lace.

A Gilded, Painted, and Carved Pine Eagle, New Hampshire, mid-late 19th century Attr. John Bellamy

Figureheads and Filigree

Early American carvers spent many a long winter whittling toys, carving figureheads for ships, and fashioning emblems of their new country for doorways and mantlepieces. Mermaids and eagles became favorite subjects—especially with a dash of bright color. The wood was coarser and the strokes cruder than Gibbons's refined fruitwood carvings, but the work of the Americans had great charm and vigor.

Hunters and Spirits

The Inuit of Canada's Arctic regions have a tradition of carving that reaches back more than 3,000 years. They work in bone, stone, tusk, antler, and wood. They carve the animals they have traditionally hunted, the hunters themselves, and the spirit beings who guide them. Inuit work is known and admired for its strong shapes and uncluttered lines. Inuit artists truly understand the nature of both the figures they carve and the materials they use.

Kimmirut Spirit with Young, Green Stone and Ivory, Ontario, Canada, 1969 Shorty Killiktee (1949–1993)

● *See also pages 18–19, 35–37, 97, 102–103*

Classical Art

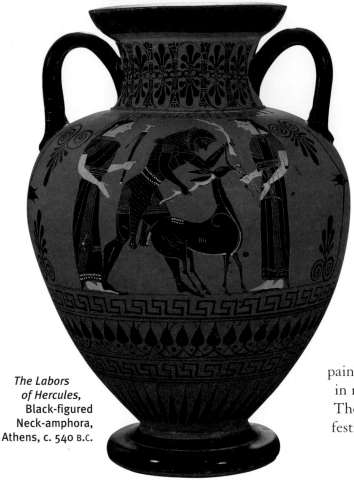

The Labors of Hercules, Black-figured Neck-amphora, Athens, c. 540 B.C.

Classical art describes the art of ancient Greece (c. 600–27 B.C.) and Rome (c. 300 B.C.–A.D. 500). During this time, architects, painters, and sculptors set standards of excellence by which Western art has been judged ever since.

From Black to Red

Most Greek painting appears on POTTERY— huge bowls and plates, tall jugs for wine and oil, and other vessels. Greek artists painted them with scenes from daily life and tales of gods and heroes. At first, the artist-potters painted in black on the red clay background (black-figure style). Later, they did the reverse, painting the background black so the figures stand out in red, like a photographic negative (red-figure style). The paintings were filled with lively details of games, festivals, and hunts—and wonderfully lifelike figures.

The Human Figure

The earliest Greek SCULPTURE was simple and stylized. Then artists began to study the human form and portray it as perfectly as they could. Even their gods were depicted as very real men and women.

Bronze Figure of a Banqueter, Greek, late 6th century B.C.

The Parthenon Sculptures

Among the best-known of all Greek sculptures were the ones made to decorate the Parthenon, the Temple of Athena on the great hill of the Acropolis in Athens. The painter and sculptor Phidias (c. 490–430 B.C.) created a series of free-standing figures and friezes (decorative bands on a building) in high and low RELIEF, filled with warriors and goddesses, horses and mythological creatures.

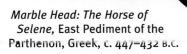

Marble Head: The Horse of Selene, East Pediment of the Parthenon, Greek, c. 447–432 B.C.

Lapith Triumphing Over a Wounded Centaur, Metope XXVII, South Side of the Parthenon, Greek, c. 447–432 B.C.

The Romans

The Romans developed the art of the PORTRAIT by making busts (head sculptures) of important people. The faces of emperors, generals, senators, and philosophers are known to us from fine portrait heads carved in stone or cast in bronze. Busts became so popular that sculptors often used standard shapes for hair, and facial features altered to suit each client. Nevertheless, the best of these uniquely Roman sculptures—with their realistic, aging faces—show great character and individuality. They are the first true portrait likenesses in art history.

The Emperor Hadrian, Cast Bronze Head, Roman, c. A.D. 117–138

● *See also pages 97, 102–104*

Collage

Pictures made from existing materials—newspapers, photographs, fabric, or flowers—combined with DRAWING and painting, and fixed to a board or canvas are called **collages**. Collage comes from the French word *coller*, meaning "to paste." It was first used in art by the cubists in the early 1900s.

Grandmother (collage of shingles, needlework, print, and pressed flowers), 1925   Arthur G. Dove

Katarinahissen (collage on paper), 1936 Kurt Schwitters

Gathering the Past

The choice of materials used in a collage sets the tone and feeling of the finished work. Mementos such as needlework and pressed flowers in *Grandmother*, by American painter and illustrator Arthur G. Dove (1880–1946), create cozy memories of past times. Kurt Schwitters (1887–1948) chose tickets, cigarette packets, and other hard-edged modern symbols to make *his* point. Schwitters, a German follower of DADA, was the first artist to use junk in his collage paintings.

Robert Rauschenberg (b. 1925)

Painter, printmaker, and designer, the American artist Robert Rauschenberg is also a great experimenter. His huge mixed-media works, which he calls "combine paintings," included elements of painting, SILK SCREEN, and collage. Starting with a flat canvas, he adds items such as bottles, clothing, clocks, and radios. In a famous work entitled *Bed*, he added blankets and pillows, too! By 1959, when Rauschenberg exhibited a stuffed goat stuck inside a rubber tire, his collages had really become free-standing sculptures.

***Untitled (collage),* undated**
Robert Rauschenberg

Collecting Culture

The use of collage in "serious" painting by the cubists sprang from their desire to show shapes in a new way. Marcel Duchamp and the dadaists used it as a kind of anti-art by creating "ready-mades"—paintings and sculpture from *objets trouvés* (French for "found objects"). The odder the materials, the sharper and wittier the comment on modern life and art. In the 1950s and 1960s, the old art of collage became the new art of assemblage. Instead of building up a textured surface in paint, artists used existing materials to create their effects—cloth, cardboard, leather, even broken POTTERY. The use of more and more three-dimensional (seen all round) objects made assemblages a new form of art. It falls somewhere between painting and SCULPTURE.

● *See also pages 32–34, 81–83, 102–105*

Color

We can see or perceive **color** because the human eye and brain react to the light absorbed by or reflected from the surface of an object. Each color absorbs or reflects light in a different way. Every color has three basic characteristics: hue—the name of the color (blue, red, orange); lightness—the amount of light reflected from a colored object (light blue, dark blue); and chroma—the intensity or concentration of color (pure blue, blue-gray). Artists create brilliant color effects by mixing the pigments (coloring powders) in many combinations.

Pope Paul III, 1543
Titian

Using color

The Venetian painter Titian (Tiziano Vecelli c. 1490–1576) has been called the founder of modern painting. He established the importance of OIL PAINTING as a medium and color as the source of both form and atmosphere. Titian handled paint with great skill—using fat brushstrokes and even his fingers to blend his favorite gorgeous colors, especially reds.

Making color

Colorants are chemical substances that give color to materials often used to produce visual art—such as paint, ink, crayons, felt-tip pens, and PASTELS. Colorants that dissolve in water are called dyes. Colorants that remain as solid particles are called pigments. When two colorants are mixed, a third color is produced. Adding black to any other color produces a shade of that color. Adding white to another color creates a tint of the color. A mixture of black and white makes gray.

Chromatic Circle of Hues by the French color theorist Michel Eugène Chevreul, published in 1839.

Red	Blue	Yellow
Red + yellow = **Orange**	*Blue + red =* **Purple**	*Yellow + blue =* **Green**

The primary and secondary colors of light are different from those of paint.

Primary colors

The three basic colors that can be mixed to form all other colors are called *primary colors in paint*.

Secondary colors

Primary colors mixed in pairs form *secondary colors in paint*.

The Dining Room in the Country, 1913 Pierre Bonnard
The Minneapolis Institute of Arts

Pierre Bonnard (1867–1947)

"I realized that color could express everything." That is how Pierre Bonnard summed up his artistic philosophy. Like the impressionists, Bonnard used pure strong color to capture and hold light in his paintings. His subjects were the world around him: his studio, lunch laid on a bright cloth, or a glimpse of garden framed in a window. An early car-owner, Bonnard explored the French countryside he loved. He captured it all in paintings filled with luminous color, bathed in light so warm the canvases almost look hot to the touch.

James Abbott McNeill Whistler (1834–1903)

A failed army career brought Whistler to Europe in his early 20s. He studied painting in Paris, but made his home in England where his style, wit, talent, and outspoken views on art made him the most famous—and notorious—American in London. Whistler is remembered as much for his quarrels as for his work. He braved ridicule and bankruptcy to establish the right of artistic freedom for every artist.

Harmony in Grey and Green: Miss Cicely Alexander, 1872–74
J.A.M. Whistler

The Butterfly

Tailpiece from
The Gentle Art of Making Enemies,
1890 J.A.M. Whistler

Whistler signed his works in a typically witty way—with a butterfly. Beginning in 1869 as a variation on his initials "JW," the signature butterfly took many different shapes over the years. Always perfectly in tune with each work, the butterflies became a symbol of their creator.

Color and Form

Whistler brought from Paris to London an admiration for Japanese COMPOSITION and an almost abstract sense of color—as well as a superb technical skill. Using thinned glazes of oil paint, he worked with the quick freshness of WATERCOLOR to capture the misty, ever-changing light of his adopted city, or the forms of his sitters. Borrowing terms from music, Whistler created "harmonies," "arrangements," and "nocturnes" of form and color.

Nocturne: Blue and Silver—Chelsea, 1871
J.A.M. Whistler

Color and feeling

The American painter Georgia O'Keeffe (1887–1986) painted deserts and shadows endlessly deep and flowers as big as landscapes in wonderful sun-drenched colors. In 1930, she said of her work, *"I know that I can not paint a flower. I can not paint the sun on the desert on a bright summer morning but maybe in terms of paint color I can convey to you my experience of the flower. Color is one of the great things in the world that makes life worth living.... Painting is my effort to create an equivalent with paint color for the world—life as I see it."*

Red Poppy No. VI, 1928
Georgia O'Keeffe

Color as content

To the painters of the twentieth century, color became even more important as a means of visual expression—to create form, atmosphere, and content. Shapes were built with color alone. Color itself often became the subject. The Russian-born American Mark Rothko (1903–70) became famous in the 1950s for painting huge, calm, wall-size canvases filled edge-to-edge with blocks of vivid color. Where colors collided, new colors appeared to dance along the horizon. This technique was often called color-field painting.

Ochre and Red on Red, 1954
Mark Rothko

● *See also pages 6–11, 32–33, 44–47, 50–55, 68–71, 73, 80, 86–87, 96, 100–101, 110–111 and 120–121*

Composition

The **composition** of a picture is the arrangement of the individual parts to form a whole. In the two-dimensional (flat) space of a painting, an artist organizes shapes, lines, and COLORS into an underlying structure. This holds the work together, whatever its style. The final composition may be symmetrical (for strength and serenity) or asymmetrical (for tension and excitement) in form.

The Baptism of Christ, c. 1460
Piero della Francesca

Piero della Francesca (c. 1415–92)

The great religious painter Piero della Francesca was ignored for centuries. Now he is recognized as one of the most important artists of the RENAISSANCE. He lived most of his long life in Umbria, away from the artistic bustle of Florence, Venice, and Rome, pursuing his love of painting and mathematics. Piero died on October 12, 1492—the very day Columbus first saw the New World. But his timeless, abstract quality remained fresh. It inspired Cézanne and the cubists—and almost every modern movement of the twentieth century.

The Legend of the True Cross: Sheba Worships the Wood / The Meeting of Solomon and Sheba, 1452–1466 Piero della Francesca

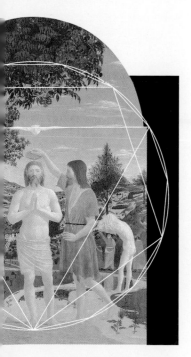

"Reading a Picture"

With his mastery of geometry and PERSPECTIVE, Piero della Francesca takes the viewer into the heart of the "story." In *The Baptism of Christ,* all of the mathematical relationships BALANCE perfectly. The figure of Christ stands at the center of an upside-down triangle. The base is formed by horizontal clouds and the outstretched wings of the hovering dove.

He is also in a rectangle, a pentagon, and a circle—central to the painting in every way.

The Legend of the True Cross

Piero della Francesca's most famous work is a series of FRESCOES at Arezzo. *The Legend of the True Cross* is a set of story paintings with many unusual features. They are placed high on the walls of a three-sided chapel, but the perspective is from the viewer's eye level. They are arranged in three vertical layers, a single band of which is shown above. And the sequence of stories has been purposely jumbled to place the pairs across from each other. The figures are gathered together within tight architectural settings, and the colors are flat and graphic.

● *See also pages 10–11, 74–75, 86–87, 92–93, 98–99*

Computer Art

Art that has been produced with the aid of a computer can be called **computer art**. It takes many forms, from computer graphics used in advertising and television to animated feature films. Computer-generated pictures are exhibited in galleries.

Geometric Art

The beauty of geometry, which is made from regular shapes—circles, squares, spheres, cones—has been appreciated since ancient times. But the shapes found in nature have always been seen as wilder and more irregular. Recently a new form of geometry, fractal geometry, has been developed. It describes the irregularities of nature. While not intended as "art," computer-generated models of endlessly repeating fractal curves make beautiful, multicolored ABSTRACT ART.

Computer-generated Mathematical Art – a 1024 x 767 Fractal Image 1985 Art Matrix

Buzz Lightyear
and Woody,
Toy Story, 1995
John Lasseter, Pixar
© Walt Disney

Characters and Special Effects

Computers are part of the modern visual world. Computer-aided design (CAD) now helps in designing everything from new model cars to space shuttles. Television commercials mix computer animation with live action to sell products. The range and sophistication of computer games gets better all the time. Not so long ago, games had simple two-dimensional (flat) shapes chasing one another across plain-colored backgrounds. Now all young gamers can follow their heroes through the detailed 3-D depths of endless imaginary worlds, and fight fantastic enemies in 256 different colors!

Some of the biggest advances in computer art have been made in feature films. What began as special effects (FX) technology to create movement and action in imaginary spacecraft now has given us elaborate fantasy worlds and full-scale dinosaurs. In 1995 came the first fully computer-animated film, *Toy Story,* created by the artists and animators at Pixar. This spectacular film won special awards, including an Oscar, for its creator John Lasseter. In 1998 Pixar did it again, with *A Bug's Life.* Their voices supplied by well-known actors, the characters came alive for delighted audiences. *Toy Story 2* followed in 1999.

Conceptual Art

In **conceptual art** the artistic idea is at least as important as the finished work of art. Conceptual art often takes the form of a "work in progress," appearing as words, performances, or activities as well as objects. The artist seeks to share with an audience the process involved in making art.

Dada in the 1960s

Among the many movements in the 1960s was a new form of anti-art. Sadly the conceptualists seemed to have much less fun than those in the DADA or POP ART movements. But, like them, they questioned the nature of both art and reality. In 1965 an American artist, Joseph Kosuth (b. 1945), exhibited a work made up of a wooden chair, a photograph of the chair, and a printed definition of the word *chair*. Which carried the true meaning of "chair"? Perhaps they all did. The viewer had to decide.

One and Three Chairs, 1965 Joseph Kosuth

The Umbrellas (Joint Project for Japan and U.S.A.), 1986 Christo

Is it Art?

In conceptual art the concept (idea) is often a question. The final form it takes may be an answer—or not. It may be a statement, a video, a stick, a hole in the ground, or a neon sign. Time may play a part—as it surely did for the artist who promised to send a postcard every day or photograph everyone in the world! Many conceptual works are as shocking and rule-breaking as those of the dadaists. Others are thought-provoking, or boring—sometimes on purpose. Some are charming, like the grand projects of the Romanian artist Christo (b. 1935) who put jolly pink skirts around small islands and marched blue and yellow umbrellas across the LANDSCAPE. The best are puzzling and make the viewer provide his or her own answer. But one question asked is always the same: "Is it Art?"

● *See also pages 20–21, 28–29, 34, 76–79, 81–83, 102–103*

Cubism

Cubism was the first movement into ABSTRACT ART of the twentieth century. It began in Paris with the work of Pablo Picasso and Georges Braque, who tried to paint three-dimensional (all-around) reality into two-dimensional (flat) space. They painted things as they were "known to be" rather than as they "appeared."

Guitars

Picasso and Braque often worked closely together. Their early cubist paintings are very similar. They used many of the same THEMES, especially the shapes of musical instruments. Their partnership lasted just seven years, but the cubist style influenced many other artists.

Woman With a Guitar, 1915 Pablo Picasso

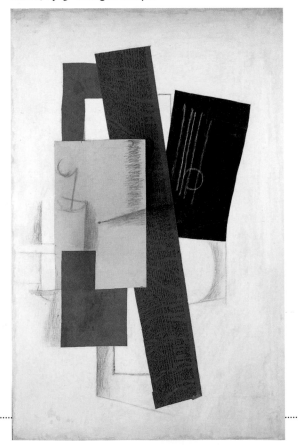

Guitar, 1913 Georges Braque

The World in Many Facets

Cubism sprang from DADA, an interest in African CARVING, and the advice of Paul Cézanne that an artist should *"deal with nature by means of the cylinder, sphere, and cone."* The cubists ignored PERSPECTIVE, depth, and rounded surfaces. They showed all facets (sides) of an object or figure at once. In their works table legs rose in the air, and two eyes appeared on the same side of a nose!

Girl Before a Mirror, 1932 Pablo Picasso

Pablo Picasso (1881–1973)

Pablo Picasso was born in Spain. He studied art in Barcelona, where his enormous talent was recognized while he was still a teenager. At 20 he had a one-man show in Paris and joined the city's artistic life. In 1907, Picasso exhibited his painting *Les Demoiselles d'Avignon*, which showed his interest in the non-naturalistic styles of African carving. It caused a sensation! He and Georges Braque used this freedom to remake form to create cubism. Throughout his long career, Picasso experimented with SCULPTURE, printmaking, and POTTERY, as well as painting. In much of his later work, cubist echoes can still be found.

Georges Braque (1882–1963)

The French painter Georges Braque was inspired by two important art exhibitions in Paris: the fauves in 1905 and the Cézanne Memorial Exhibition in 1907. The free use of COLOR in FAUVISM and Cézanne's experiments with form led to Braque's own vivid use of color and distorted (altered) forms. His meeting with Picasso brought these ideas into sharper focus. Together they established cubism, which remained a lifelong interest.

Instruments de Musique et Compotier, 1919 Georges Braque

● *See also pages 6–7, 20–21, 26–27, 90*

# Dada

Dada was the first anti-art movement. It began in Switzerland in 1916, with a group of young poets and artists who rebelled against the horrors of World War I. Dada had no rules, it was the art of protest. The artists threw away all traditional values in their work. They concentrated instead on the absurd and outrageous. Their aim was not to please, but to shock.

Nude Descending a Staircase, No. 2,
1912 Marcel Duchamp

"Destruction is also Creation"

The dadaists met regularly at the Cabaret Voltaire in Zurich. Led by the Romanian poet Tristan Tzara(1896–1963), they produced wild entertainments. They involved their audiences in impromptu (unrehearsed) "performance art." Chance played a part in everything. Even the name *dada* was chosen at random (as a baby-talk word, or from the Slavic words for "yes! yes!"). The unsettled postwar mood helped to spread the movement throughout Europe and America.

Marcel Duchamp (1887–1968)

The Frenchman Marcel Duchamp became leader of the New York dadaists. He created "ready-mades"—SCULPTURES made from mechanical parts. They looked like machines, but could not work, and had no purpose. He created a sensation at the New York Armory exhibition of 1912 with his painting *Nude Descending a Staircase, No.2*. It portrayed not a rounded figure in space, but the *action* of the figure as it moved down the stairs. This early work became one of the great icons of early twentieth-century art. It influenced dada artists in Europe and the United States.

● *See also pages 20–21, 32–33, 62–63, 81–83, 114–115*

Decorative Arts

When useful objects are designed or decorated to make them pleasing to look at, they fall under the heading of **decorative arts**. This describes both applied arts—furniture, fabrics, books—and ornamental items such as jewelry and some types of POTTERY.

Egyptian Decoration

The ancient Egyptians loved decoration on walls, floors, clothing, and furniture. They started making wooden furniture over 4,000 years ago. From the beginning it was beautifully made. The tombs of the pharaohs (rulers of Egypt) were filled with furniture and treasure chests. Each piece was carved and painted, inlaid with gold and precious stones. The chests held coins for the journey to the afterlife. Amulets (charms) to bring good fortune were based on the glittering wing cases of sacred scarab beetles.

Pectoral Jewel with Heart Scarab, Egypt, 19th Dynasty c. 1275 B.C.

Whistling Pots

Ever since people first discovered that containers made from baked clay were both useful and attractive, potters have been experimenting with unusual shapes and COLORS. The highly skilled potters of the Peruvian coast of South America created pots for many uses—and sometimes just for fun. This wide-eyed, 1,000-year-old owl has a whistle inside his hollow head!

Whistling Vessel in the Form of an Owl, Peru, A.D. 800–1200

American Decorative Art

When the first settlers from Europe arrived in the New World, they brought with them examples of the arts and crafts of many cultures. Borrowing from them all, in time they created a new, uniquely American style.

Patchwork Art

For centuries needlework of all kinds was both a necessity and a form of artistic expression. It became even more so for the European women who settled in America beginning in the 1600s. Wooden houses to fill and the long harsh winters spurred them on to great creativity. They designed clothes, painted and decorated furniture, created STENCIL designs on walls and floors, and made rugs from scraps of fabric. The rise of a local cotton-printing industry made possible the most highly prized of all the needlework crafts: the American patchwork quilt. It was made from pieced or appliquéd (overlaid) printed cottons in an endless variety of designs and colors.

Mennonite "Star of Bethlehem" Patchwork Quilt, Pennsylvania, late 19th century

Familiar and Festive

Many objects for daily use in nineteenth-century American homes were made from cast iron or galvanized tin. They came in the uncheerful colors of black or silver-gray. Painting them with fruit and flower motifs in bright colors on a glossy black background turned them into handsome, decorative items, which gave a festive look to ordinary kitchens.

Painted Tea Caddy and Coffeepot, Pennsylvania German, 1810–40

Art Nouveau

Art nouveau (French for "new art") became an international style in design and decoration from 1890 to 1915. Popular throughout Europe and America, the style was based on the asymmetric (unbalanced), curving lines of plants. It was used in book design, interior decoration, pottery, and architecture. But every innovation is built on history. One of the forms used by art nouveau designers was the "arabesque"—borrowed from Islamic art. It is a curling, elongated shape, also based on natural forms. It had been a favorite motif of Islamic potters for a thousand years.

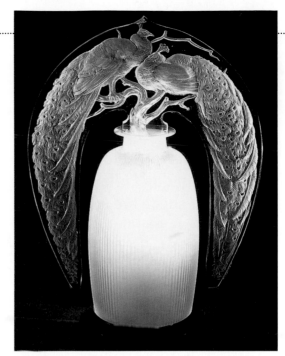

Glass Lamp, undated René Lalique

The Willow Tea Rooms,
Sauchiehall Street, Glasgow, 1903
Charles Rennie Mackintosh

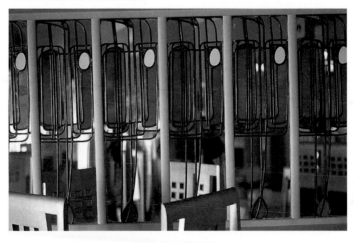

The Art Nouveau Flower

The most important architect of the art nouveau style was the Scot Charles Rennie Mackintosh (1868–1928). He designed everything from the building itself to the candlesticks on the table. In his most famous designs—for the Glasgow School of Art, The Hill House (home to a children's book publisher and his family), and the Willow Tea Rooms—he used the exaggerated flower forms of art nouveau, and introduced the crisp geometry of squares and circles that would become the basis of the art deco style of the 1930s.

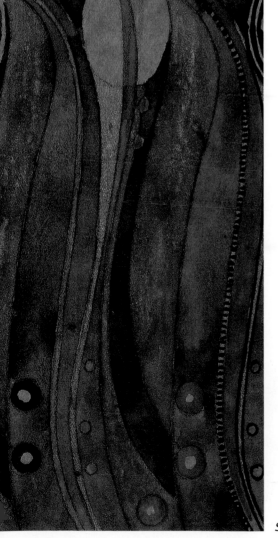

Stylized Tulips (Design for Silk), c. 1918–23 Charles Rennie Mackintosh

● *See also pages 16–17, 20–21, 52–53, 60–61, 88–90, 108–111, 117, 122–123*

Drawing

Drawing is the art of creating an image in line only, and often in just one COLOR. Areas of shade are suggested by cross-hatching (small lines laid over one another). Western artists draw with many things: charcoal, pencil, chalks, or pen and ink. Eastern artists often use brushes and ink.

Brushstrokes

To Chinese and Japanese artists, painting and drawing have traditionally been the same thing. They used the same tools—ink and brushes— for both. Professional artists could use a brush to make many different strokes, which bring to life the LANDSCAPES of another time: a twisted tree trunk, with spiky needles or rustling leaves; solid, ever-rising cliffs; slow, rolling swirls of water. Long thin scroll shapes helped to give unusual depth and PERSPECTIVE to these beautiful brush drawings.

Retreat Deep in the Mountains (Hanging Scroll), 1753 Zhang Zongchang (1686–1756)

Sketching

Drawings are sometimes done as sketches to prepare for paintings, prints, or SCULPTURE. They sometimes seem more fresh and original than the later works based on them, as if the "spirit" of the subject has been caught best in the quick, early drawing. In the hands of the greatest draftsmen they are themselves works of art.

Three Women and a Child, (sketch for sculpture) 1944 Henry Moore (1898–1986)

Studies of Horses, c. 1490 Leonardo da Vinci

Leonardo da Vinci (1459–1519)

The Florentine Leonardo da Vinci was among the first artists of the RENAISSANCE to work from observing life around him. In everything he did, Leonardo was curious and enthusiastic. He investigated subjects very deeply. Leonardo made careful studies of nature. He tried to understand its exact forms in every detail: plants, animals, rocks, and rushing water. He loved horses, trained them with kindness and patience, and studied their movements until he could draw them perfectly.

Leonardo followed people in the street, making quick sketches of faces, hands, feet, and gestures. He learned anatomy (how bodies are made) by dissecting (cutting apart) corpses. The Florentine historian Georgio Vasari said, *"To Leonardo we owe a greater perfection in the anatomy of the horse, and the anatomy of man."* Leonardo da Vinci was also a scientist and inventor. He filled many notebooks with his thoughts on PERSPECTIVE, anatomy, PROPORTION, and COMPOSITION, all written in tiny mirror writing.

● *See also pages 12–15, 42–43, 52–53, 58–59, 94–96, 100–101, 120–121, 124*

Earth Art

Earth art began in the late 1960s as a reaction against technology and a renewed interest in nature and the environment. Artists worked with natural materials: rocks, soil, water, leaves, branches—and the LANDSCAPE itself. Many of their works depended on space, remote uninhabited places, and the passage of time for their effects. Earth art is often ephemeral (short-lived). It exists in a lasting form only in photographs.

The Effect of Time

Many works of earth art are huge—trails of stones across many miles, earthworks, and even reshaped volcanoes. One of the most famous is the *Spiral Jetty* by Robert Smithson (1938–73). In 1970, Smithson arranged 7,000 tons of crushed rock into a huge spiral shape 1,500 feet long in the polluted shallow waters of the Great Salt Lake in Utah. It was a powerful image in a ruined landscape—slowly disappearing as the murky waters rose. In two years it was gone.

Andy Goldsworthy (b. 1956)

Andy Goldsworthy is an English sculptor who uses as his raw materials chosen landscapes and the natural forms that can be found nearby at a particular place and time. He uses living trees, dead branches, fallen leaves, stalks, stones, snow, and even dust. These are built into arches and columns, arranged in circles, bent around holes, or laid out carefully in color-graded patterns to create works of haunting beauty. Some are made in hours. Others are built and changed over many days. Some remain for a long time. Others fade immediately—like the endless processes of change in nature itself.

Small White Granite Circles, 1984 Richard Long

Circles of Stones

Richard Long (b. 1945) is a British artist who makes geometric shapes in real landscapes using stones, paper, and grass. He creates works both big and small—cairns (stone piles) and circles of stones along a mysterious trail or arranged with perfect precision in an art gallery. They are carefully recorded in photographs.

The Art of Nature

Many of the monumental works of earth art are meant to last for years, slowly changing over time. Others are created out of delicate natural materials—arrangements of leaves and flowers, shapes made of twigs and snow—and have a shorter life. They are valued because, like so many things in nature, they are temporary. This strand of earth art reflects ROMANTICISM, the view of nature celebrated by J.M.W. Turner and John Constable in the eighteenth century.

Crack Line Through Leaves, 1986
Andy Goldsworthy

● *See also pages 30–31, 56–57, 76–79*

Engraving

In **engraving**, a design is cut into a metal plate. This creates an image from which a print in ink can be taken. Engraving grew from the skills of armorers who decorated metal armor and cannon. Line engraving, etching, drypoint, mezzotint, and aquatint are types of engraving.

Sunshine After Rain, Colored Engraving, 1816 Humphry Repton (1752–1818)

Cutting a Line: Engraving

In all engraving, lines are incised (cut) into the surface of metal with shavers or burins (pointed steel tools). Ink is forced into the cut lines. It is transferred to paper in a printing press. This is called intaglio printing. It is the opposite of RELIEF cutting, where everything except the drawing is cut away.

Albrecht Dürer (1471–1528)

Engraving was a perfect medium for illustration. It reached its peak as the most popular art form in sixteenth-century Europe with the work of the German artist Albrecht Dürer. Dürer was clever, curious, and a great draftsman. In 1495 he set up his workshop in Nuremberg. He produced an enormous body of work, both paintings and books of WOODCUTS and engravings that established him as the greatest graphic artist of his day.

Samson Fighting the Lion, Line Engraving, 1498 Albrecht Dürer

Etching and Drypoint

Etching uses a plate coated with resin (a sticky gum). A DRAWING is made with a stylus (a fine needle). The plate is dipped in acid, which "bites" the cut lines into the metal. Darker areas are created by leaving the plate in the acid longer. In drypoint the plate is not dipped in acid, so the burr (rough edge) of the cut is not polished away. This gives a soft, deep effect to the print.

The Three Trees, Etching with Drypoint, 1643
Rembrandt van Rijn

Rembrandt van Rijn (1606–69)

The great Dutch artist Rembrandt was the master of etching. After his wife, Saskia, died in 1642, Rembrandt began to sketch in the countryside. He could draw with anything: reed pens, sticks, the end of his brush, or an etching stylus. He combined his love of nature and his understanding of chiaroscuro (use of light and dark) to create a series of magnificent etchings of the Dutch LANDSCAPE.

Aquatint

Like etching, aquatint also uses acid. A porous covering is put on the plate, which allows acid to bite through in a series of tiny dots. The artist then covers each area in turn—from lightest to darkest—before the plate is dipped into the acid bath. This creates sharp-edged areas of tone that can be used to build richly colored prints.

The Letter, Aquatint, 1891 Mary Cassatt
The Metropolitan Museum of Art,
gift of Paul J. Sachs 1916: photo © 1991 M.M.A

● *See also pages 38–39, 58–59, 68–69, 84–85, 105, 108–109, 120–121, 124*

Expressionism

In **expressionism**, the artist's ideas, imagination, and feelings are emphasized. Form and COLOR are exaggerated and distorted (changed in shape) to convey the artist's thoughts and feelings. This gives a work a subjective (as experienced or sensed) rather than an objective (observed) reality. Expressionism became an important movement in the visual arts in Europe, especially in Germany, in the early 1900s.

Early Influences

The work of the German religious painter Mathis Grünewald (c. 1475–1528) is often called "expressionist." He filled his great altarpieces with crooked, blood-spattered figures to express grief and suffering. The thin, elongated, and unnaturally pale saints in the paintings of the Spanish master El Greco (1541–1614) have also been called expressionist. Both used distortion and unreality to express pity, terror, or inner strength. But the greatest influence on twentieth-century expressionists was Vincent van Gogh (1853–90). His use of intense color, simple forms, and strong rhythms inspired later artists, among them Munch and Kokoschka.

The Starry Night, 1889 Vincent van Gogh

Edvard Munch (1863–1944)

The Norwegian painter and printmaker Edvard Munch had an unhappy childhood. His mother and elder sister both died, and his father went mad. *"Illness, madness, and death were the black angels that kept watch over my cradle,"* he said. Those black angels remained with him for years, part of his life and his art. Munch's work is filled with passion, vigor, and pain—in a frenzy of swirling lines and clashing colors. Everything he saw was touched with his own raw feeling, and captured in line and tone.

Girls on a Bridge, c. 1902 Edvard Munch

Color and Movement

The Austrian-born painter Oskar Kokoschka (1886–1980) remained true to his expressionist roots throughout his long working life. He was influenced by the events of his time, including the two world wars, when his paintings were darker. Later, his colors became warmer and his subjects more mellow in tone.

Capriccio (Tales in the Forest), 1943 Oskar Kokoschka

● *See also pages 46–47, 68–69, 86–87, 100–101*

Fauvism

Fauvism was among the first new movements in European art in the twentieth century. Artists such as Matisse and Vlaminck broke away from a naturalistic style toward a greater freedom in both form and COLOR. When a group of artists exhibited their work in 1906, their bright, busy paintings looked strange. One French critic pointed to a RENAISSANCE-style SCULPTURE in the gallery and said *"Donatello parmi les fauves!"* (Donatello among the beasts!). The name stuck, and fauves they became.

Paysage, undated Maurice de Vlaminck

Maurice de Vlaminck (1876–1958)

Born into a Flemish family in Paris, Maurice de Vlaminck was an unusual and independent artist. He was against formal teaching, and remained untrained, painting for love while he supported himself by playing the violin and racing bicycles! Although he prided himself on never studying the past, Vlaminck went to an exhibition of the paintings of Vincent van Gogh in 1901. This changed his life. From then on, pure color, strong movement, and thick brushstrokes became a trademark of his fauvist paintings.

Henri Matisse
(1869–1954)

In the early 1900s, Henri Matisse began to use color in a new way. Rather than merely describing, or "recording," a subject in its actual colors, Matisse used areas of vivid, flat color and sharp, springy line to create decorative effects and atmosphere. He used this new freedom in wonderfully fresh STILL LIFES and paintings of LANDSCAPES and even people. With his love of the exotic, his superb DRAWING and eye for color, Matisse was one of the most original and important artists of the twentieth century.

Still Life With Sleeping Woman, 1940 Henri Matisse

● *See also pages 22–25, 32–33, 44–45, 68–71, 86–87, 102–104*

Foreshortening

Foreshortening is when an artist uses the rules of PERSPECTIVE to paint or draw an object or figure in space to give the appearance of depth. The full length of the subject appears condensed (shortened) to give the impression that it exists further back "inside" the space of the picture.

Andrea Mantegna (c. 1431–1506)

Andrea Mantegna was an Italian painter and engraver. He admired the work of the sculptor Donatello. In his paintings and FRESCOES, Mantegna tried to reproduce the hard surfaces of sculpted stone and cast metal. His COLOR was quiet, but the shapes were solid, the DRAWING excellent, and the spaces endless. Mantegna made his figures step "outside" the painted framework of his pictures into the real world. We feel as if we are looking into his pictures and sometimes as if we are standing close to groups of painted watchers—a spooky feeling!

Dead Christ, 1490 Andrea Mantegna

The Illusion of Depth

One of Mantegna's most striking paintings is *Dead Christ.* The pale figure of Jesus lies on a slab of stone. The tone is almost monochrome (one color). The sadness of the mourners is clear—it is a picture of bitter grief and loss. But it is the COMPOSITION that has made the painting so famous. We stand at the feet of the dead man, looking back into the picture along his foreshortened legs to the bony chest and large head. This extreme use of PERSPECTIVE draws the eye to the heart of the subject—the face of Christ.

The Ceiling of the Bridal Chamber, Ducal Palace, Mantua, 1465–1474 Andrea Mantegna

Angels on the Ceiling

In 1465 Mantegna began work on a series of unusual frescoes for the powerful Gonzaga family of Mantua. On the ceiling of the Bridal Chamber in their palace, he painted a trompe l'oeil (French for "deceives the eye") in which he opened the view to the sky. Ladies peer over the edge of a balcony, from which large birds and heavy vases seem ready to fall. Fat putti (winged cherubs) teeter on a tiny ledge high above the ground. The central image is set in a circular garland within a square frame. Everything is painted in precise foreshortened detail—but nothing is real.

● *See also pages 50–51, 74–75, 94–96, 98–99, 102–103*

Fresco

Fresco (fresh) is the technique of painting with water-based pigment (coloring powder) onto a layer of still-wet plaster. When the plaster dries, the COLOR becomes a permanent part of the finished surface. Fresco was perfected in fourteenth-century Italy, and was used by many artists of the RENAISSANCE. The most famous fresco painting was created by Michelangelo for the ceiling of the Sistine Chapel in Rome.

Michelangelo (1475–1564)

Michelangelo Buonarroti—painter, sculptor, poet, and architect—was one of the most influential artists in history. His patrons (supporters) included the powerful Medici family in Florence and the popes in Rome, but he remained an independent spirit—a restless and moody genius. Michelangelo spent his long life working to achieve perfection in his art.

The Sistine Chapel Ceiling, 1508–12
Michelangelo

The Creation of the Sun and the Moon and the Plants on Earth

The Bible in Pictures

In 1508, Pope Julius II gave Michelangelo a mammoth task—to decorate the ceiling of the papal chapel. For four years, working almost alone, he painted his vision of the Old Testament stories in nine large rectangular panels down the length of the huge vaulted space. At its center he placed the story of the creation of Adam and Eve, and their expulsion from the Garden of Eden.

The Prophet Isaiah

Prophets, Sibyls, and Architecture

Michelangelo painted columns and arches around the panels of the Sistine ceiling, and filled the space with CLASSICAL and biblical figures. Around the edges he placed twelve prophets and sibyls (seers). He used FORESHORTENING to make both the architectural details and the human figures appear in correct PERSPECTIVE to the viewer.

The Delphic Sibyl

● *See also pages 48–49, 74–75, 98–99, 102–104*

Illumination

Decorating religious texts to create beautifully illustrated manuscripts is called **illumination.** These early books combined CALLIGRAPHY (decorative handwriting) and miniature paintings filled with many details. Painted in rich COLORS on vellum (specially prepared animal skin), the ornamented capital letters, figures, and fantastic border patterns were often highlighted with gold and silver.

Monastic Life

In the Middle Ages, skillful monks in European monasteries brought Bible stories to life in beautiful illuminated manuscripts. One of the greatest is the *Book of Kells.* It is the work of many Irish monks. The *Book of Kells* is noted for the magnificent decoration of its opening words and initial letters.

The Opening Words of St. Luke's Gospel: The Book of Kells, Irish, c. 800

Everyday Life

The *Luttrell Psalter* is a book of psalms (sacred songs) in the English style of illumination. Its lively borders are filled with scenes of everyday country life through the four seasons. Its pages show the customs and activities of a real fourteenth-century village.

Luttrell Psalter, English, 1340

Courtly Life

The most striking illuminated manuscripts of all were called Books of Hours—collections of prayers for special occasions throughout the year. They were created by professional illuminators such as the Limbourg brothers (Active 1400–16), who worked for the dukes of Burgundy. Their masterpiece was *Les Très Riches Heures du Duc de Berry* with miniature paintings for each month. There were scenes of noble figures in elegant costumes, grand buildings, and perfect landscapes, all painted in bright, glowing colors.

August: Les Très Riches Heures du Duc de Berry, French, 15th century Pol de Limbourg

April and May: calendar pages from a Book of Hours, Flemish, 16th century Simon Benninck

● *See also pages 12–13*

Impressionism

When a group of French painters exhibited their work in Paris in 1874, they were laughed at. These very individual artists had turned away from the art taught in art schools. They were interested in painting everyday life, studying the effects of light on COLOR, and capturing the "impression" of a scene with quick freshness out of doors. They were called "impressionists" by the mocking critics. But **impressionism** became one of the most revolutionary and successful movements in the history of art.

Woman with a Cat, 1880–2
Edouard Manet

En Plein Air

Impressionism began in France in the 1860s, when artists began to go out of their studios and work *en plein air* (French for "in the open air"). They studied and painted natural light as it fell on colored surfaces, and the many-hued shadows that it cast. Never black or gray, the color of shadow changes according to the color of the object casting the shadow.

La Récolte des Foins (Bringing in the Hay), 1887 Camille Pissarro (1830–1903)

Les Meules (Wheatstacks),
1890–91 Claude Monet

Claude Monet (1840–1926)

Claude Monet chose a few motifs (repeating subjects or THEMES) and painted them often at different times of day. Portable painting equipment allowed him to work on large canvases outdoors, recording the scene as the light changed. But it wasn't easy. While working on his *Wheatstacks* series in the low winter light, he wrote, *"I am working away at a series of different effects, but at this time of year, the sun sets so quickly that I can't keep up with it."* The more he saw the tiny changes caused by shifts in the light, the longer each effect took to paint.

"Light and Shadow Never Stand Still"

Monet loved the movement of light on water, the shifting reflections of poplar trees, flowers shimmering in the sun, and London in the fog. He never stopped trying to capture the effects of light on color. In his beautiful garden at Giverny, near Paris, Monet created his own, ever-changing subject matter, which he studied and painted for forty years. In 1907 when his great Water Lily paintings went on show, the critic Georges Meusnier said, *"Nature, at the call of the painter, has come in person to place herself on the canvas."* Monet became the most famous and sought-after of the impressionists. Reproductions of his work can be found all over the world.

Water Lillies I, **1905 Claude Monet**

● *See also pages 22–25, 44–47, 56–57, 68–71, 73, 80, 100–101, 110–111*

Landscape

Landscape in art is the representation of natural scenery in an artistic form—as DRAWING, painting, ENGRAVING, or COLLAGE. Nature has been stylized, idealized, and abstracted by many artists throughout the ages. For others, truth in nature can only be found in the most accurate and detailed study of all its forms.

Landscape as Background

In fifteenth-century RENAISSANCE Italy, painters began to set religious scenes and figures against the real landscape. Instead of the flat gold backgrounds or idealized landscapes of the past, painters brought the stories of saints and prophets to life by placing them in the familiar settings of day-by-day existence.

A detail from *The Conversion of Saint Hubert,* 1450–85
The Master of the Life of the Virgin

Landscape at Arleax-du-Nord, 1871–74
Jean-Baptiste-Camille Corot

...as Foreground

The painters of the nineteenth-century ROMANTIC movement took nature itself as their subject—close up and real. The French painter Camille Corot (1796–1875) painted a series of *études* (studies) of nature in delicate, mid-tone COLORS recording the smallest shifts in color and shape of light on rustling leaves or waving grass.

The Hay-Wain, 1821 John Constable

Homely and Familiar

John Constable (1776–1837) loved the landscape of the English wetlands in which he grew up—the light and shade, the effects of wind and rain, and the great cloud-filled skies. He set out to paint them as accurately and "scientifically" as he could. His informal COMPOSITIONS are filled with the homely props of everyday country life.

The Wild Majesty of Nature

The vast wilderness of the American continent fascinated artists of the Old World, who had never seen it. Painting it as it was, the German-American painter Albert Bierstadt (1830–1902) showed the world a landscape of natural power and beauty—still untouched by the human hand.

Sunset in the Rockies, 1866
Albert Bierstadt

● *See also pages 22–25, 54–55, 98–101*

Lithography

Lithography (Greek for "to draw with stone") is a method of printmaking. A picture is drawn with a grease pencil on the surface of a stone. The stone is washed with water. Because oil and water don't mix, oily printing ink sticks only to the drawing. When paper is pressed to the stone, a print—in reverse—appears.

A New Medium

Lithography was invented in 1798 by Aloys Senefelder (1771–1834). As the story goes he was making a laundry list and used a grease pencil on a piece of stone! Soon, many artists saw the possibilities of lithography. It suited the fluent drawing style of the great French artist Honoré Daumier (1808–79). Most of his work was produced in the form of lithographs. Their soft images carried his biting satires on French society.

The Legislative Paunch, 1834 Honoré Daumier

"Reine de joie...", 1892 Henri de Toulouse-Lautrec

Henri de Toulouse-Lautrec (1864–1901)

Henri de Toulouse-Lautrec was a man of independent spirit and overflowing talent. Teenage injuries affected the growth of his legs but not his career or busy social life. Toulouse-Lautrec was a wonderful draftsman and became an expert in lithography. His love of the work of Japanese WOODCUT artists influenced his own print technique. He used flat, transparent areas of COLOR, strong outline drawing, and asymmetrical (unbalanced) COMPOSITIONS. His brilliant series of posters advertising Parisian night spots popularized both posters and lithography.

Cirque Teriade, Paris, 1967 Marc Chagall

Marc Chagall (1887–1985)

Marc Chagall was a Russian artist who spent much of his life in France. Poetic images of his Russian homeland, his family, animals, and flowers float through his paintings. *"Is it not true that painting and color are inspired by love?"* he asked. His life was often harsh, but his inspiration and joy never failed. In many of his paintings a kindly guardian angel watches over the scene. Chagall also worked in OIL PAINTING and WATERCOLOR, gouache, STAINED GLASS, and ceramics. He designed sets for theater and ballet, TAPESTRIES, book illustrations, and MOSAICS. In 1933 he did a series of lithographs to illustrate *The Arabian Nights,* creating new effects of color. It was the first of many sets of prints on THEMES including Bible stories, folk tales, and the circus.

● *See also pages 64–65, 68–71, 88–90, 106–107, 117, 120–121*

Masquerade

A **masquerade** is a celebration, dance, or performance where decorative masks and costumes are worn. Throughout history and in many cultures, there have been rituals, religious ceremonies, plays, and entertainments in which stylized masks disguise the wearers' true identities.

Shira-Punu Mask,
Carved and Painted Wood, traditional, Gabon, Africa

New Ireland Spirit Mask,
Shells, Wood, Fibres, and Painted Teeth, traditional Pacific Islands

Tala-Wipiki, Lightning Kachina Doll,
1891 Hopi Indians

Ritual Dances, Masks, and Dolls

Dancing is one of the oldest forms of celebration. In prehistoric times people celebrated important occasions in large flowing circle dances. Dancers often wore masks in the shape of people, animal heads, gods, or monsters. They believed these masks held a power or magic that the dancer could also experience. Lion and dragon dances, in which many dancers become part of a single animal with a giant papier-mâché head, are very old rituals used to celebrate the Chinese New Year. Masks and headdresses also play an important part in the ceremonial life of North American Indians. They work with local materials: painted wood, animal skins, woven grasses, beads, and feathers. The tribes of the Pacific Coast made double masks—one face that of an animal, the other human. Hopi Indians use carved and painted kachina dolls representing various spirits of earth and sky in their dances.

Stylized Theater

The actors in ancient Greek drama disguised themselves with large masks representing gods, familiar characters, or feelings (gladness, anger, sorrow). Actors in traditional Japanese theater use elaborate costumes, wigs, dance, and slow, stylized gestures to tell stories from the history and mythology of Japan.

The Kabuki Actor Ichikawa Kodanji,
1856 Utagawa Kunisada (1786–1865)

Skeleton Angel and Devil Drinking, **Mexico,**
20th century Leonardo Linares

The Day of the Dead

On November 2 each year Mexico celebrates the Day of the Dead, when the dead are remembered and honored. During this slightly macabre (gruesome) festival, presents are exchanged, special food is prepared, and people take to the streets for a carnival of music and dancing. The symbols of the day are everywhere—sugar skulls, little papier-mâché devils and skeletons, as dancing figures, lacy paper cutouts, or fantastic costumes on revelers in the street.

Mobile

A **mobile** is a form of SCULPTURE that moves. The carefully balanced parts of a mobile are constantly rearranged into an endless variety of random shapes in space, propelled by the gentle movements of the air. Invented in the early 1930s by American sculptor Alexander Calder, the mobile became an important twentieth-century modern art form.

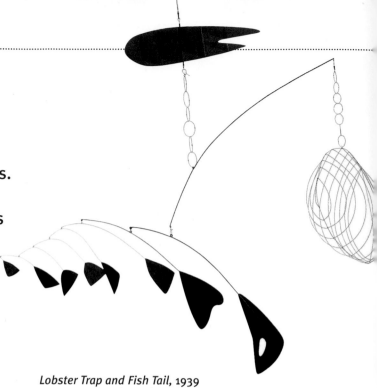

Lobster Trap and Fish Tail, 1939
Alexander Calder

Trophy of Chasse-Le-Golem, 1990
Jean Tinguely

Balance

Alexander Calder created his first mobile in 1932. He cut shapes out of sheet metal and suspended them from wire rods so that they remained in perfect balance. These painted shapes might be leaves, stars—or fish. The hanging shapes move, making an ever-changing series of "new" sculptures in space—but they are never out of balance. In the mobile above, the fish never ends up in the trap.

Kinetic art

Mobiles are just one form of kinetic art—art that involves movement. Mobiles move naturally. Other kinds of kinetic art are designed to move unnaturally. They may rattle or shake, turn from side to side or up and down. Many works by the Swiss sculptor Jean Tinguely (1925–91) were created from scrap materials and powered by little electric motors. These humorous examples of the machine age were the opposite of Calder's beautiful, silent mobiles.

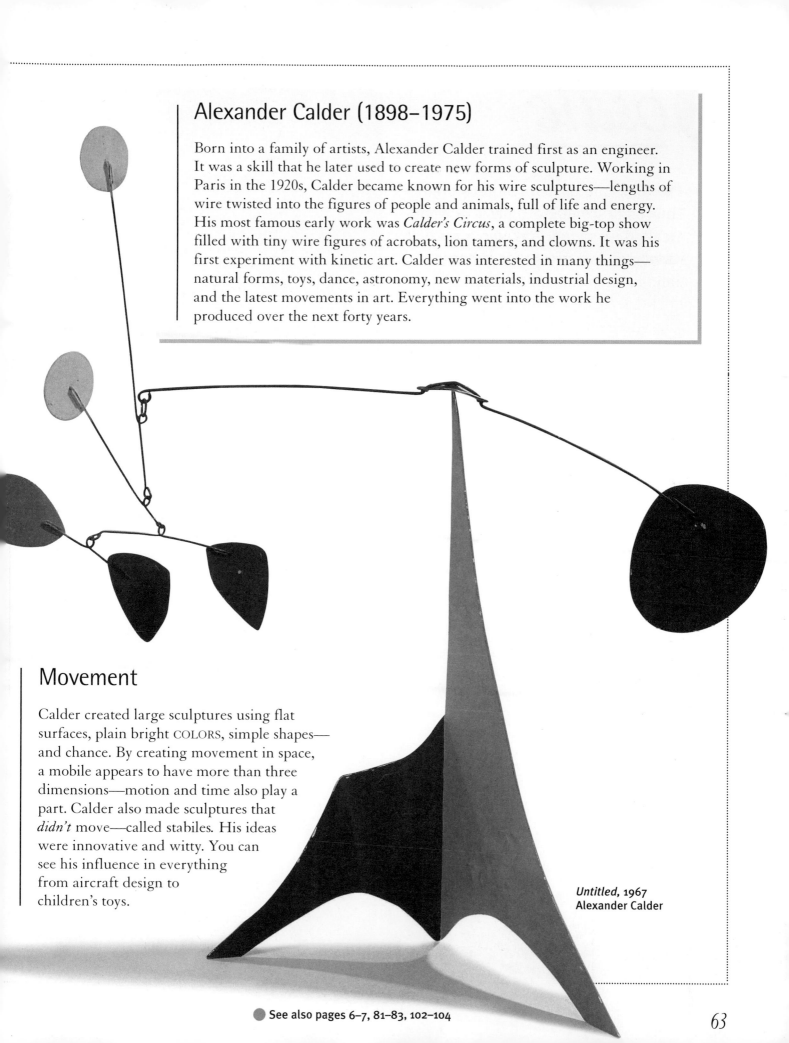

Alexander Calder (1898–1975)

Born into a family of artists, Alexander Calder trained first as an engineer. It was a skill that he later used to create new forms of sculpture. Working in Paris in the 1920s, Calder became known for his wire sculptures—lengths of wire twisted into the figures of people and animals, full of life and energy. His most famous early work was *Calder's Circus*, a complete big-top show filled with tiny wire figures of acrobats, lion tamers, and clowns. It was his first experiment with kinetic art. Calder was interested in many things— natural forms, toys, dance, astronomy, new materials, industrial design, and the latest movements in art. Everything went into the work he produced over the next forty years.

Movement

Calder created large sculptures using flat surfaces, plain bright COLORS, simple shapes— and chance. By creating movement in space, a mobile appears to have more than three dimensions—motion and time also play a part. Calder also made sculptures that *didn't* move—called stabiles. His ideas were innovative and witty. You can see his influence in everything from aircraft design to children's toys.

Untitled, 1967
Alexander Calder

See also pages 6–7, 81–83, 102–104

Mosaic

Mosaics are made of multicolored pieces of stone, clay, glass, or wood (called *tesserae*). The pieces are arranged into scenes or patterns and fixed in cement or plaster.

Bellerophon Slaying the Chimera, Mosaic Floor, Lullingstone Roman Villa, Kent, 4th century A.D.

Roman Floors

Mosaics date from over two thousand years ago. Roman architects created durable mosaic floors for public buildings and the courtyards of grand country villas. Archaeologists have uncovered mosaics that are still colorful after centuries, even after being buried by lava. Many feature mythological scenes or details of plants and animals, surrounded by patterned borders.

Aztec Ornament

Aztec artists of the sixteenth century used mosaic differently. Instead of decorating floors or walls, they created small ornaments covered with tiny chips of semiprecious stones, especially the brilliant blue turquoise of Mexico.

Turquoise mosaic pectoral ornament, Mixtec-Aztec 1400–1520

The Palace, Wall Mosaic, Sant'Apollinare Nuovo, Ravenna, 6th century

Dovelets, Mausoleum of Galla Placidia,
Ravenna, 5th century

Byzantine Ceilings

The early Christians borrowed the Roman technique of mosaic to decorate their churches. It was used most effectively in the beautiful churches of the Byzantine Empire. Mosaic pictures cover the walls and high vaulted ceilings—the symbols of heaven—made in tiny squares of deep blue and gleaming gold.

Symbolic Animals

Plants and animals appear in mosaic designs in every era. Sometimes they are symbols, sometimes they are just themselves. Mediterranean fish swim beside mythological creatures; real plants grow between rows of saints; mystic lambs gaze down from golden pastures. Fifth-century doves—Christian symbols for the soul—are recognizable today in the doves of peace in this twentieth-century mosaic by Fernand Léger (1881–1955).

Les Oiseaux sur Fond Jaune, Central panel,
mosaic facade, Musée National Fernand Léger,
1955 Fernand Léger

Mural

A **mural** is a wall painting. It may be painted directly onto the surface of the wall—as a FRESCO is—or painted on a panel fixed to a wall. In some murals, trompe l'oeil (French for "deceive the eye") is used to create an illusion of greater space. In others, the large flat areas are used for crowded scenes.

Accompanying the Dead

Like people in many cultures, the ancient Egyptians believed in life after death. Wealthy and important people made many careful preparations for their journey into the afterlife, including building special tombs. Great pyramids were built to house the burial chambers of the pharaohs (kings) of Egypt. The mummified bodies were placed in stone coffins and surrounded by treasure, figures of servants, religious texts, and even food. The walls and ceilings of the small chambers were covered with murals showing happy scenes of daily life. Families prayed to the god Osiris, hoping to bring the scenes as well as the person to life.

A Banquet with Musicians and Dancers, Wall Painting, Tomb of Nebamun, Egypt, Eighteenth Dynasty c. 1390 B.C.

Diego Rivera
(1886–1957)

Diego Rivera, the great Mexican painter and muralist, was an artist from the beginning. By the time he was four, his father had made him a studio—a room with canvas-covered walls on which he could draw as much as he liked—to protect the rest of the house. Rivera was rebellious, stubborn, and very bright. He graduated from high school at the age of twelve. In the 1920s the work of Rivera and the Mexican muralists attracted the attention of artists all over the world. Combining local masonry skills with traditional European methods, they reinvented the art of fresco painting. Murals became an important expression of Mexican art in the twentieth century.

Friday of Sorrows on the Santa Anita Canal, from *A vision of the Mexican People,* Mural Cycle in the Ministry of Education, Mexico City, 1923–24 Diego Rivera

Celebrating Life and History

Rivera loved politics and the history and art of Mexico. They came together in his greatest works—the series of murals he did for public buildings in Mexico City. These showed the history and struggles of the Mexican people from the time of the great Aztec civilization. Rivera believed that all art belonged to the people. It should be seen, free, in public places. He showed that art sprang from the daily life of ordinary people. It could be used to tell a powerful story and teach useful lessons.

● *See also pages 14–15, 26–27, 48–51, 91–96, 112–113*

Oil Painting

For **oil painting**, pigments (coloring powders) are mixed with a binder of linseed oil. Artists thin the COLORS for use with a medium of oil, varnish, and turpentine. Oil painting became popular in the sixteenth century. It is still the most common fine art technique.

Brushwork

Working in oil shows an artist's personal style of brushwork. Color can be built up slowly with thin washes (called glazes), or laid on thickly and quickly with brushes, knives, or fingers. Oil paint is slow-drying. Colors can be blended to make a smooth surface.

Sir Peter Paul Rubens (1577–1640)

Peter Paul Rubens, a Flemish artist and diplomat, became one of the most important people of his time. He spoke six languages and traveled widely. More rarely, he was a great painter who was hugely successful during his life. His style was lush. He painted huge canvases filled with larger-than-life characters. They hung in the palaces of royal patrons (supporters) all over Europe. Helped by many assistants, Rubens produced paintings, ENGRAVINGS, interiors, decorations, TAPESTRIES, and books.

The Supper at Emmaus, 1601 Caravaggio

Caravaggio (1571–1610)

The young Michelangelo da Merisi—known as Caravaggio, the town of his birth—brought the Venetian style of painting to Rome in 1592. Working directly onto canvas, he painted swift studies from life. His PORTRAITS, religious scenes, and small STILL-LIFE pictures are dramatic, with rich colors and deep shadows. He attracted notice—and disapproval—for his life and work. But Caravaggio's direct, unfussy use of oil paint had a lasting effect on the painters of the seventeenth century and later.

The Head of Cyrus Brought to Queen Tomyris
c. 1622–23 Peter Paul Rubens

Chiaroscuro: Light and Shade

The term chiaroscuro (from the Italian words for bright and dark) describes an artist's use of contrasting tones of light and shade. Explored with oil paint by Caravaggio and the painters who followed him, chiaroscuro was used most effectively by the Dutch artist Rembrandt (1606–69). Rembrandt used areas of high, light colors and strong, deep shadows to give depth and feeling to his oil paintings, painted in warm earth colors. He also used chiaroscuro in his drawings and ENGRAVINGS in black and white.

Portrait of the Artist's Mother, c. 1629 Rembrandt van Rijn

Thomas Gainsborough (1727–88)

Thomas Gainsborough was a famous English painter of portraits and LANDSCAPES. The English aristocracy hired him to paint family portraits— cool, elegant celebrations of themselves lounging in front of their mansions. Gainsborough admired many painters, especially Rubens, but he developed his own painting style. He built up the surface of a picture with small, feather-light daubs of color. His tones were warm and pearly—blues and greens, peach, yellow, and dusty pink. Many painters had assistants with a special talent for painting the rich clothing and draperies of their wealthy sitters. But Gainsborough had no assistants. He painted the folds of taffeta, sheen of silk, and soft pile of velvet better than anyone. His real love was landscape, which he painted for pleasure, while painting portraits for a living.

Mr. and Mrs. William Hallett "Morning Walk", 1785 Thomas Gainsborough

● *See also pages 10–11, 22–25, 46–47, 54–57, 84–87, 94–96, 98–101, 110–111*

Impasto

When an artist uses oil paint in thick strokes, unmixed with other colors or thinned with medium it creates an effect called impasto. The marks left in the paint by the brush or knife can be seen clearly. It is one of the ways in which experts can identify the work of a particular artist. The technique of impasto painting was often used in IMPRESSIONISM by painters such as Pierre-Auguste Renoir (1841–1919) and Mary Cassatt (1844–1926). They used impasto to paint fresh flower petals, young girls, and plump sofa cushions.

Glaieuls Dans un Vase Bleu,
undated Pierre-Auguste Renoir

Young Lady Reading, **undated Mary Cassatt**

Op Art

In the early 1960s, artists began to experiment with optical illusions, or tricks of the eye. They created paintings and SCULPTURE in which the lines, shapes, and COLORS were arranged with perfect precision—and small differences. The surfaces seemed to dance before the eye. Reviewers labeled it **op(tical) art**.

Orient IV, 1970
Bridget Riley

Geometry and Illusion

The world discovered op art in 1965 through a New York art exhibition called "The Responsive Eye." Two stars emerged. One, Victor Vasarely (1908–97), was an experienced Hungarian-born French painter who created pictures in flat, contrasting colors. The other, the English artist Bridget Riley (b. 1931), filled huge canvases with crisp, ordered shapes that seem to shimmer and wave. Fashion and graphic designers in the 1960s borrowed many images from their work.

Piros-EG, 1972
Victor Vasarely

● *See also pages 6–7, 116*

Pastel

Pastels are DRAWING sticks made from powdered pigments. Pastels are often used with colored paper. They are applied dry—in strokes of heavy COLOR or blended on the surface to create areas of soft, shaded tones.

Dream Flowers

The French symbolist painter Odilon Redon (1840–1916) used pastels with great skill and imagination. These flowers in a vase glow with sparkling color. They look almost like jewels.

Vase of Flowers, pastel on paper, 1914 Odilon Redon

At the Milliner's, 1882 Edgar Degas
The Metropolitan Museum of Art, bequest of Mrs. H.D. Havemeyer, 1929.
The H.O. Havemeyer Collection. Photo © 1987 M.M.A.

Edgar Degas (1834–1917)

The French artist Edgar Degas was one of the great draftsmen of his time. His paintings were shown alongside those of the impressionists, but his subjects were all his own: days at the races, evenings in cafés and theaters, backstage at the ballet and the circus. Degas used pastels often, and very well. His pastel drawings on colored papers have the richness of OIL PAINTING and the lightness of WATERCOLOR. But Degas planned every detail. *"Even when working from nature,"* he said, *"one has to compose."*

● *See also pages 22–25, 38–39, 54–55, 68–69, 120–121*

Perspective

Perspective is a way of suggesting a three-dimensional (all-around) space on a two-dimensional (flat) surface. It comes from a Latin word meaning "to look through." Artists in many cultures have developed different ways of suggesting perspective.

Depth and Distance

Mathematical perspective was invented in the fifteenth century by the Florentine architect Filippo Brunelleschi (1377–1446). He organized shapes in space—showing that they seem to become smaller as they move away from the viewer.

Paolo Uccello (1397–1475)

A painter who loved animals and filled his studio with pictures of birds, Paolo Uccello's name means *"bird."* His huge, busy paintings show his other lifelong passion—perspective. In this painting, the lines of lances, legs of prancing horses, bodies of fallen soldiers, and the tiny figures on the hill beyond all point toward the heart of the battle.

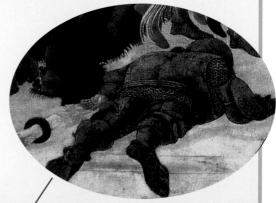

The Battle of San Romano, 1454–57 Paolo Uccello

A Boy Handing a Woman a Basket in a Doorway, c. 1660–63
Pieter de Hooch

Vanishing Point

A straight road running into the distance seems to disappear at a single point on the horizon. But as we travel along, the point where the road vanishes from sight is always just ahead. It is an illusion created by moving through three-dimensional space. Artists can make this feeling of depth by using perspective. In pictures, the "vanishing point" is the point where parallel lines seem to meet at the horizon.

Pieter de Hooch (1629–84)

The great Dutch artists of the seventeenth century used perspective best in scenes of daily life in houses. Pieter de Hooch and Jan Vermeer (1632–75) were the most skillful painters of this "interior space." You can follow the lines of windows, rooftops, rooms beyond doorways, and—most of all—the patterns of tiled floors back to their vanishing points. De Hooch set out the points—often two or three—with pins and string on the canvas before he began to paint.

● *See also pages 10–11, 26–27, 32–33, 48–51, 56–57, 92–99*

Photography

Photography (Greek for "to draw with light") is the art of making pictures with light. A camera focuses the light reflected from an object onto light-sensitive paper, or film. Chemicals are used to produce a lasting image of the object. Photography was developed in France and England in the early 1800s. Since then, it has become one of the most popular visual art forms.

"The Open Door", Plate VI in *The Pencil of Nature*, 1844 William Henry Fox Talbot

Does the Camera Ever Lie?

It is often said that the camera never lies. But from the very beginning photographs have been arranged or posed to make a particular point. Subjects were chosen as carefully as they would be by a painter. When photography was new, they had no other guide. One of the pioneers of photography, the Englishman William Henry Fox Talbot (1800–77), created the first photographic picturebook, *The Pencil of Nature*, in 1843–44. He said his scenes of country life were *"formed or depicted by optical and chemical means alone ... impressed by Nature's hand."* Early photographers believed Nature was in charge of this new, mysterious process. The photographer could "take"— but not "make"—the picture.

Summer Day, Portrait Photograph, 1850s
Julia Margaret Cameron (1815–79)

Abraham Lincoln, c. 1860–61 Mathew Brady

The Reality of Battle

The mid-nineteenth century saw the birth of "news" or "documentary" photography, when cameras first went to war. The British photographer Roger Fenton (1819–69) took the first pictures of battlefields ever published when he covered the Crimean War (1853–56). The American Civil War (1861–65) was photographed by the fearless Mathew Brady (c. 1823–96) and his assistants. They went into the heart of the fighting with a wagonload of equipment. A sad but resolute Abraham Lincoln (1809–65) sat for several portraits during the war—the first American president to be photographed. Pictures captured the formalities of army life: the neat camps and the ranks of soldiers drawn up for inspection. But they also showed the horror of battle itself, and the poor living conditions that caused so many deaths from disease. War photography has been shaping public opinion ever since.

Dragoon Guards,
The Crimea,
c. 1855
Roger Fenton

*Dunes, Oceana,
California*
**Silverprint, 1936
Edward Weston**

Canal, Holland, **Silverprint, 1971 Brett Weston**

Nature in Black and White

The first "travel" photographers lugged heavy equipment down rivers and up mountains to bring back images of wild LANDSCAPES to people comfortably at home. The American West provided many of the most striking landscapes ever photographed. It offered photographers such as Edward Weston (1886–1958) the pure, clean vision of a bleak but beautiful country, which suited his technique of "straight photography." His work was echoed years later in the work of Paul Strand (1890–1976) and Ansel Adams (1902–84). Later, Weston's son Brett (1911–93) also responded to the geometry of landscape. They stripped their subject down to line and form, light and shade, and reproduced its strength and timelessness in black and white alone.

Reality and Illusion

From its beginning photography never became part of the main body of fine art. It was the work of individuals or small groups of people in different areas, some commercial, some artistic. Most photographic work was commissioned.

The work of many great photographers first appeared in the pages of popular magazines such as *Picture Post, Vogue, Life, National Geographic,* and *Vanity Fair,* not in specialist publications or beautifully framed in a gallery.

In Search of Times Past, **Photo Collage, 1959 Herbert Bayer**

The Museum: Two Female Statues and Boy Looking at One of Them, **undated Henri Cartier-Bresson**

Capturing the Moment

Photography is an art of instant response to world events or private dramas. The French photographer Henri Cartier-Bresson (b. 1908) captured such frank moments with a miniature camera. Photography reflects back to us who and what we were at any time since its invention 175 years ago.

Pointillism

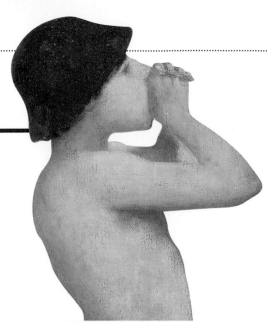

The French artist Georges Seurat painted small, rounded spots of pure COLOR, precisely placed on his canvas. When seen from a distance this created the illusion of natural colors and solid forms. This technique became known as **pointillism**, from a French word meaning "mark with dots, or points."

Georges-Pierre Seurat (1859–91)

Born in Paris, Georges-Pierre Seurat studied at the famous École des Beaux-Arts. He liked the THEMES of holiday life found in IMPRESSIONISM, but not the impressionists' casual manner. Seurat tried a more scientific approach to the study of light and shade. He worked out his own painstaking and precise method of applying dots of pigment that "blended in the eye" to create a dazzling display of color. His paintings had great depth of space, strong contrasts, and bold COMPOSITION. However, people thought they lacked the freshness of the impressionists. Seurat died at the age of just 31, but he had a lasting influence on the artists who followed him.

Bathers at Asnières, 1883–84 Georges-Pierre Seurat

● *See also pages 22–23, 54–55*

Pop Art

Pop art was a movement based on consumerism in America and Britain. It uses images from popular culture—advertisements, TV, and comic books. In pop art works of art were "packaged" just like other things in consumer societies.

Campbell's Chicken Rice Soup Box,
1986 Andy Warhol

Soup Art

Pop art painters and sculptors used images of favorite products. They also used commercial art techniques, such as SILK SCREEN and photolithography, and industrial materials—aluminium, plaster, acrylics, and plastics—for their work.

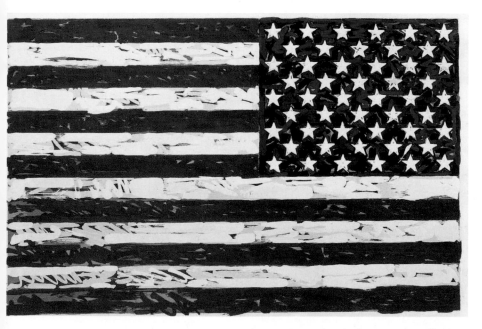

Flag (Not in F.; Not in Ulae), 1973 Jasper Johns

Symbols as Art

The American flag—the "Stars and Stripes"—is a famous cultural symbol. Flags are seen so often that they are almost taken for granted. In the 1950s, an American painter, Jasper Johns (b. 1930), used the flag in his work. By making the flag an art object, Johns had changed the way people viewed it.

Pop Art

The Adventures of Valentine Vox the Ventriloquist, 1974
Peter Blake (b. 1932)

The City of the Circle and the Square,
1963–66 Eduardo Paolozzi (b. 1924)

The Sixties Revolution

In music, fashion, design and art, the 1960s became the decade of pop. American museums showed the work of artists such as Andy Warhol, Jasper Johns, and Roy Lichtenstein. The familiar images and bright colors were a welcome change from the ABSTRACT ART of the 1950s. Pop art found collectors at once. Like the images from the world around them, pop paintings and SCULPTURE became instant consumer favorites!

Pop in Britain

The term that best described the art of the 1960s came from London. In 1956, the English artist Richard Hamilton (b. 1922) first used the word *pop* in a collage. He predicted that pop art would be *"Popular (mass market), Transient (short term), Expendable (easily forgotten), Low-cost, Mass-produced, Young, Witty, Gimmicky..."* It was all of those things, on both sides of the Atlantic.

Two Cheeseburgers with Everything (Dual Hamburgers), 1962 Claes Oldenburg

Claes Oldenburg (b. 1929)

If the hamburger is recognized everywhere as a symbol of American culture, then Claes Oldenburg's big double helping is one of the great icons (symbols) of pop art. The Swedish-born American grew up in Chicago. He was inspired by junk food—and once filled a rented shop with sculptures of every product. He said, *"The hamburger is a perfectly structural piece of food and I think I'd rather look at it than eat it."*

Comic Strips

Roy Lichtenstein (b. 1923) produced some of the most popular pop art paintings. His huge dot-by-dot recreations of images appeared to come from action and love-story comics (the "Splat!!" and "Oh, Brad..." school of painting). His images were, in turn, used on posters, tee shirts, and postcards. They had come full circle as inexpensive products to buy.

Crying Girl (b.4), 1963 Roy Lichtenstein

● *See also pages 20–21, 105*

Portrait

Images of people are called **portraits**. An artist may present the head, half body, or full figure of the subject. The person may be standing, sitting, or lying down. Whatever the pose, a portrait is more than a "likeness" of a person. Something of the subject's character must come through in the finished work.

Self-portrait at the Age of 63, 1669
Rembrandt van Rijn

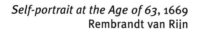
The Duke of Wellington, 1812-14 Francisco de Goya

The Self-portrait

Over the years, Rembrandt searched his own face for expression and meaning. He produced more than seventy self-portraits, making his face one of the most famous in art. All human faults are there, caught by the greatest of all portrait painters. He stares out at us from under strange hats and unkempt hair, growing old before our eyes.

The Heroic Portrait

When the brilliant Spanish artist Francisco de Goya (1746–1828) painted the duke of Wellington, he showed a man in his prime, on the offensive in his long military campaign against the French. The straight back, the direct gaze, and the medals proudly worn all show a person of importance and purpose—the public figure rather than the private man.

John Singer Sargent (1856–1925)

John Singer Sargent was an American who lived in Europe, drawing inspiration from both cultures. His portraits detailed the lives of European aristocrats and rich Americans in a grand, lush style. Sargent's paintings were of glamorous subjects but done with great craftsmanship.

The Daughters of Edward Darley Boit, 1882
John Singer Sargent

The Family Portrait

Sargent's most famous painting of a family is unlike his other elegant family portraits. Four girls are shown in a large, dark, almost empty room. It is an *Alice in Wonderland* world of children in an oversized setting. The smallest child floats on a vast, sea-colored rug. The tallest is dwarfed by an oriental vase. Its bold COMPOSITION, muted COLORS, and unsentimental gaze make this one of Sargent's greatest "subject" pictures.

Paul Helleu Sketching with his Wife, 1889
John Singer Sargent

The Informal Portrait

Portraits aren't always posed. A portrait can be an impression, painted in swift, bold strokes. It might capture a moment when the subjects don't even look up—happy, busy, and unaware of our interest.

● *See also pages 26–27, 44–47, 50–51, 54–55, 58–59, 68–71, 76–77, 98–99, 102–104*

Post-Impressionism

In the late nineteenth century many artists began to turn against IMPRESSIONISM and follow new styles of painting. Among them were Paul Cézanne, Paul Gauguin, and Vincent van Gogh. Their art was called **post-impressionism** (*post* means "after.") At first, critics and public alike rejected their work.

From Light to Form

The French painter Paul Cézanne (1839–1906) said he wanted *"to make of Impressionism something solid and enduring, like the art of the museums."* Instead of studying light reflected from the surfaces of solid forms, he wanted to paint the forms themselves. He tried to understand the underlying structure of objects.

Madame Cézanne in a Red Armchair, c. 1877
Paul Cézanne

Still-Life with Ginger Jar, Sugar Bowl, and Oranges, 1902–06
Paul Cézanne

Among Cézanne's favorite subjects were objects on a table, figures sitting in chairs, and the LANDSCAPE of his beloved Provence in southern France. His work had a great effect on twentieth-century painting. In 1914 the English critic Clive Bell called Cézanne *"the Christopher Columbus of a new continent of form."*

Vincent van Gogh (1853–90)

The Dutch painter Vincent van Gogh trained for the church. He worked among the poor, often giving them his own possessions. But his true calling was in art. During the last ten years of his life, van Gogh produced over 800 paintings—and sold just one! In spite of illness, this intelligent, thoughtful artist poured out his ideas on art and life in hundreds of letters to his brother, Theo. The intense feeling expressed in his paintings, and his life, have made van Gogh one of the most revered artists of all time. His once unwanted paintings now sell for record-breaking sums.

Houses at Auvers, 1890 Vincent van Gogh

Paul Gauguin (1848–1903)

Paul Gauguin rejected naturalistic painting in favor of a more graphic approach to COLOR. This unusual French artist grew up in Peru, and loved exotic lands and ancient cultures. In 1891 he traveled to the Pacific island of Tahiti. He filled his pictures with the tropical lushness of this beautiful land. His bold DRAWING, flattened forms, and warm colors make patterns that fizz and zing across the surface of his paintings.

Nave Nave Moe (Sacred Spring), c. 1894 Paul Gauguin

● *See also pages 26–27, 44–45, 54–55, 68–69, 80, 84–85, 110–111*

Pottery

Pottery is a name given to objects made of fired (baked) clay. Pottery-making is one of humankind's oldest skills, dating from the Late Stone Age, about 8000 B.C. Potters decorate their work with natural COLORS and incised (cut) patterns.

Earthenware and Stoneware

There are two main types of pottery, earthenware and stoneware. Earthenware is thick and roughly textured. It is opaque—you can't see through it. Fired at low temperatures, at first it is porous. But it becomes waterproof when it is covered with a layer of slip (glaze) and refired. Earthenware armies to accompany a dead emperor to the afterlife have been found in burial chambers in China. Stoneware is made of finer clay. It is fired at higher temperatures, which gives it a glassy surface.

Porcelain Covered Vase, Lung-ch'uan ware, Sung Dynasty, Chinese, 12th–13th century

Tomb Figure of a Horse, Tang Dynasty, Chinese, A.D. 700–750

Porcelain bowl painted in Kakiemon-style enamels, Japanese, c. 1670–90

Porcelain

Porcelain is made from fine white china clay (called kaolin) and fired at a very high temperature. It is extemely hard, and so thin light can pass through it. The Chinese discovered how to make it about A.D. 700–800. They created works of great beauty. Potters in other countries were inspired by Chinese porcelain.

Four tiles, Persian Flower Design, Utrect, c. 1885

Tiles and Bowls

Geometric and leaf-patterned tiles made by Islamic potters decorate some of the world's most beautiful buildings, from the great mosques of the Middle East to the Taj Mahal in India. Stylized green and blue flowers are characteristic of bowls from Iznik in Turkey.

Iznik Fritware Bowl, Turkish, c. 1540

Lusterware Majolica Plate "I will love whoever will love me." Italian, Castel Durrante, c. 1535

Figurines

In the eighteenth century, skillful modelers in Germany created small porcelain figures as ornaments. They made dancers, clowns, shepherdesses—figures of every kind, alone and in groups. Colorful, lifelike, and charming, these small figurines are great favorites with collectors of ceramic objects.

Majolica

Because they had no kaolin clay, Islamic potters invented majolica, a new type of tin-glazed earthenware. It is pure white and glossy, making a perfect surface for decoration in rich metallic colors, such as manganese-purple and copper-green. Masterpieces of decorated majolica were created by Italian artists of the sixteenth century.

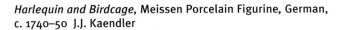

Harlequin and Birdcage, Meissen Porcelain Figurine, German, c. 1740–50 J.J. Kaendler

Pottery

Studio Pottery

While machine production brought china to every table, the tradition of the artist-potter remained strong. Using the age-old techniques of molding, incising, glazing, and firing, artists continue to create pieces of "studio pottery"— ceramic works of art that have little useful function.

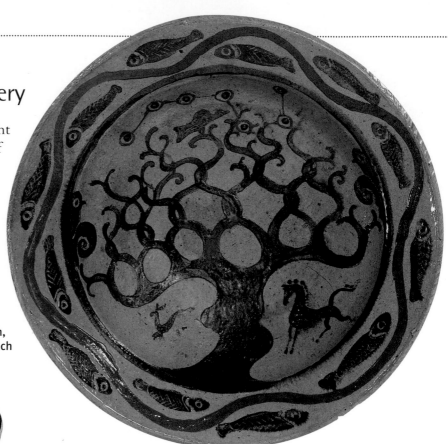

The Tree of Life, Earthenware Dish, 1923 Bernard Leach

Large Bird with Black Face, Earthenware Pot, 1951 Pablo Picasso

Form, Function, and Fun

Pottery can be used as a base for paintings and SCULPTURE. Pablo Picasso covered plates with lively bullfighting scenes, and used the shapes of vases and jugs for comical, fat-bodied birds. Sometimes the function of an object suggests the form—eggs nestle inside Kaarina Aho's covered dish.

Egg Dish and Cover in the Shape of a Hen, Finland, Kaarina Aho for Arabia 1952

● *See also pages 18–19, 35–37*

Prehistoric Art

Prehistoric art dates from the time before written records were kept. Small stone, bone, and ivory SCULPTURES remain from that time. Preserved in caves or buried in the earth, they are treasured relics from the Early Stone Age, 20,000–30,000 years ago.

La Dame de Brassempouy, Mammoth Tusk Ivory Head from Grotte du Pape, France, 21,000 B.C.

Cave Art

Early prehistoric hunters painted pictures of the animals they hunted. They are found on the walls of huge limestone caves, including Altamira in Spain and Lascaux in southern France. Painted in swift strokes in strong, natural COLORS, the pictures provide a lifelike record of prehistoric animals.

Bison, Cave painting, Altamira, Spain, c. 14,000–10,000 B.C.

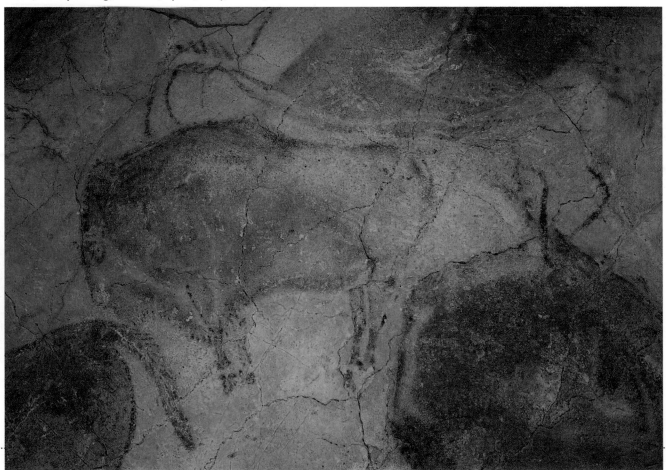

Proportion

The rules of **proportion** are about the sizes and positions of the parts of a work of art. The parts relate to each other, and they also relate to the whole picture. Proportions can be worked out using mathematical calculations. Some artists use their eyes to judge sizes and shapes.

Man of Perfect Proportions,
(Vitruvian Figure), c. 1490
Leonardo da Vinci

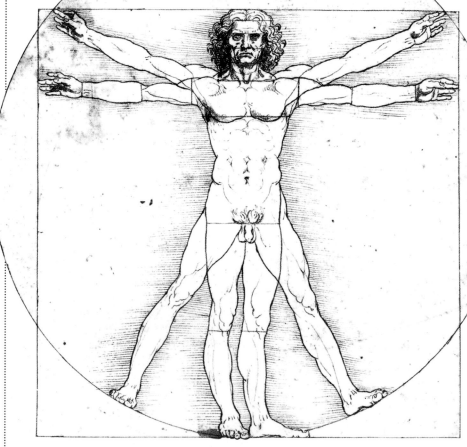

The Vitruvian Figure

The ideas of the Roman architect Vitruvius (c. 50 B.C.) were studied by the artists and architects of the RENAISSANCE. In his famous book, *De Architectura* (On Architecture), he states that a man of perfect proportions standing upright with outstretched arms will make a square shape; and with arms raised and legs apart, will make a circle. This image became an important symbol of harmony. The great artist Leonardo da Vinci's example is the best-known version.

The Feast in the House of Levi, 1562
Paolo Veronese

Paolo Veronese (c.1528–1588)

Paolo Veronese was an outstanding artist in sixteenth-century Venice. His finest works were huge FRESCOES for grand public buildings. He got in trouble with the church for painting a biblical scene, *The Marriage at Cana,* as a lively Venetian feast. Veronese explained that *"we painters use the same licence as poets and madmen."* (The church let him rename the painting *The Feast in the House of Levi.*) The vast architecture seems to dwarf the richly dressed guests— all except the calm figure of Christ at its heart.

Eight Heads High

Renaissance artists liked to measure proportions exactly. They used standard measurements to create perfect proportions for figures and buildings. For example, the perfect body stands eight heads high, as shown in da Vinci's Vitruvian figure.

● *See also pages 38–39, 48–51, 74–75, 98–99, 102–104*

Realism

In **realism,** or naturalism, people and objects are represented as they are seen in life. From the artists of Classical Greece, through the Renaissance to the nineteenth century, artists searched for ways of portraying people and objects in a natural way.

Gustave Courbet (1819–77)

In nineteenth-century France, artists created a new art of the ordinary. They looked for truth, not beauty. Gustave Courbet, the leading realist painter, said, *"Painting ... consists of the presentation of real and existing things."* The critics hated his work, so Courbet showed it outside the official gallery. His skill and rebellious spirit strongly influenced other painters.

For the Track, c. 1895
John Frederick Peto (1854–1907)

Trompe l'Oeil

Trompe l'oeil is a French phrase meaning "deceive the eye." Artists try to make the viewer believe that the highly detailed painting of an object is as real as the object itself. Popular since Roman times, trompe l'oeil has often been used with humor—to create the illusion of space in small rooms, or play a gentle joke with a carefully placed fly on the nose of a sitter.

Still-Life: Apples and Pomegranates, 1871–72 Gustave Courbet

American Naturalists

In the nineteenth century, American painters created a particularly American style of "warts-and-all" realism, making pictures of the emerging life and character of the new country. Among the greatest of the American naturalist painters was Thomas Eakins (1844–1916). A difficult man but a great teacher, Eakins made careful studies of the human figure—through anatomy and PHOTOGRAPHY, as well as DRAWING from life. Eakins set out to capture the bustling activity of nineteenth-century Philadelphia. He admired action and sport. A keen rower, he painted other oarsmen propelling their little crafts lightly over the surface of the water. In the painting below, everything is clean and precise: the small wooden boat, the colored reflections on the rippling water, the stretched muscles of a rower on a warm summer day.

John Biglin in a Single Scull, 1873 Thomas Eakins

Trodden Weed, 1951 tempera on panel
Andrew Wyeth Collection of Andrew
and Betsy Wyeth
Copyright Andrew Wyeth

Andrew Wyeth (b. 1917)

The American painter Andrew Wyeth comes from a famous family of artists. His father was a noted illustrator and his son is also a talented painter. During his long career, Wyeth has created a haunting series of perfectly observed images of the countryside around his home. He is among the few modern painters to master the centuries-old method of tempera painting, in which pigments (coloring powders) are mixed with egg yolks (pale ones are best). Tempera COLORS are natural, earth colors—like the dry, spare tones of his native LANDSCAPE. *"Winter* is *that color here in Pennsylvania,"* he said.

Wyeth's paintings are noted for their sharp detail. In some, you can almost feel the different textures of fur, feathers, grasses, or stones. In others, a few swift strokes of color create a shape on the page. Suddenly white paper has become a heavy fall of snow. But this is not photographic realism. Wyeth picks and chooses each detail, which the camera cannot. *"I search for the realness, the real feeling of a subject, all the texture around it,"* he said.

● *See also pages 10–11, 26–27, 48–49, 54–57, 68–71, 74–79, 98–99, 110–111, 114–115, 118–121*

Relief

Relief CARVING is SCULPTURE in which details stand out from a background. They are seen from one side only. Figures carved almost completely round are in high relief. Figures that are not cut very deep are cut in low relief.

The Emperor Augustus, depicted as a god shortly after his death, Sardonyx Cameo, Roman, C. A.D. 14–20

Ivory, Wood, and Stone

Relief carvings are made in any hard, durable material, such as stone, hardwood, or ivory. From prehistoric times, artists all over the world have carved in ivory. The Romans made miniature relief carvings in gemstones to create beautiful cameos. They are still made and prized today.

The Gates of Paradise

In 1402, the Italian Lorenzo Ghiberti (c. 1378–1455) won a competition to create a pair of doors for the Baptistry of Florence Cathedral. His design had twenty-eight panels of relief sculptures. Each panel was molded, cast in bronze, and gilded (covered with gold). Later, he made ten more panels. Ghiberti spent 50 years on the work. They were the finest relief sculptures ever made. Michelangelo praised them as worthy to stand as the *"Gates of Paradise."*

The Gates of Paradise, 1425–52 Lorenzo Ghiberti

The Deposition, Ivory Carving, English, School of Herefordshire, 1150

● *See also pages 16–17, 102–103*

Renaissance

Renaissance means "rebirth." It refers to the great period of artistic creativity that began in Italy in the fourteenth century. It was marked by a return to classical style in architecture, and naturalism in art. This flowering of the arts had long-lasting influences.

The Classical Past

Renaissance thinkers returned to the ideals of ancient Greece and Rome. They celebrated the power and dignity of human beings. Their ideas were based on humanism (the study of man) rather than theology (the study of God). Their religious paintings of real people in natural settings were fresh and joyful compared with the stiff, stylized medieval art.

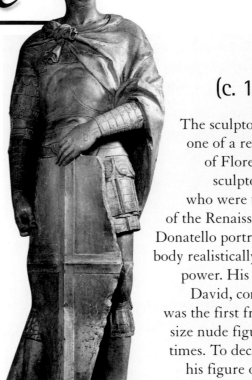

St. George, 1416 **Donatello**

Donatello (c. 1386–1466)

The sculptor Donatello was one of a remarkable group of Florentine architects, sculptors, and painters who were the true creators of the Renaissance style in art. Donatello portrayed the human body realistically and with great power. His bronze statue of David, completed in 1430, was the first freestanding, life-size nude figure since ancient times. To decorate the base of his figure of St. George, he invented a kind of RELIEF CARVING (seen from one side only) so delicate that the Florentine historian Vasari called it *"DRAWING in stone."*

The Annunciation, c. late 1450s
Fra Filippo Lippi (c. 1406–69)

Hunting on the Lagoon, c. 1490 Vittore Carpaccio

Vittore Carpaccio (c. 1460–c. 1525)

The Venetian painter Vittore Carpaccio was a skillful and imaginative storyteller. He painted the lives of saints and the legends of heroes, often creating whole series of pictures to tell their stories. Like other Renaissance painters, he explored the rules of COMPOSITION and PERSPECTIVE. He built strong frameworks for his narratives—like stage scenery set up for the action of a play. His enchanted visions became records of Venetian daily life.

Raphael (1483–1520)

Raffaello Sanzio, known as Raphael, was the son of a painter. He was sent to study with the finest teachers of his day. By the age of 20 Raphael had completed his first commissions. He established his reputation with his great FRESCO, *The School of Athens*. Raphael's PORTRAITS have soft outlines, warm rich COLORS, and a luminous strength. By the end of his short life Raphael was firmly established as one of the greatest painters of the Renaissance—the "Best of the Best."

The Lady with the Unicorn, c. 1510–20 Raphael

● *See also pages 10–11, 14–15, 18–19, 26–27, 38–39, 48–51, 56–57, 68–71, 92–93, 97, 102–103, 118–119*

Romanticism

In **romanticism**, imagination and feelings were favored over reason and order. Artists and writers rebelled against the formal style of the early eighteenth century. Romanticism was an important movement in England and France from about 1790 to about 1860.

Color and Movement

The most important of the French romantic painters was Eugène Delacroix (1798–1863). Delacroix traveled in Spain and North Africa. He painted sun-drenched LANDSCAPES, costumed figures, dashing soldiers on prancing horses, and muscular, graceful wild animals. He captured action and feelings in swift oil sketches.

Cavalier Turc, c. 1825 Eugène Delacroix

In a Shoreham Garden, 1829
Samuel Palmer

In Praise of Nature

Romantic poets and painters believed nature was a living spirit. They thought Mother Nature was older, wiser, and deeper than well-ordered society. Everything "natural" was good, and human rules stifled the romantic spirit. Artists were inspired by the poetry of William Wordsworth (1770–1850) and the paintings of John Constable (1776–1837). Samuel Palmer (1805–81) painted even small landscapes in dramatic curlicues of black line and frothy puffs of COLOR with white accents.

The Picturesque

J.M.W. Turner (1775–1851) painted the landscape itself. He loved the effects of light on rushing water or rugged ground. Even an ordinary country scene had its ruined castle, perfectly placed on the horizon in hazy afternoon light. It was a romantic reminder of a grander past.

Hornby Castle, undated
J.M.W. Turner

The Wanderer Above The Mists, 1818
Caspar-David Friedrich

Mystical Landscape

The romantics loved the notion of faraway places, either real or imaginary. The German romantic painter Caspar-David Friedrich (1774–1840) combined this with an interest in the supernatural to create extremes of romantic landscape painting. His imagined world was dark and bleak. It was filled with sharp-edged crags and cold mists swirling over vast spaces. He did not seek to harmonize sad nature and the lonely figures pitted against it. The ideas of romanticism attracted the rebel. Friedrich's strangely powerful pictures seemed to favor the loner against the world.

● *See also pages 56–57* 1062940828

Sculpture

Sculpture refers to freestanding works of art that can be seen from all sides. Generally made from durable materials—stone, wood, bone, steel, clay, plastic—sculptures have a timeless presence. The earliest sculptures had a magical or religious importance. It is an art form still used to express spiritual or symbolic ideas.

The Venus of Willendorf,
Stone figure,
c. 30,000–25,000 B.C.

Prehistoric Sculpture: People and Animals

PREHISTORIC ART from the Stone Age includes beautiful little CARVINGS of human figures and animals in ivory or bone. Prehistoric artists also modeled in clay and sculpted in stone. The goddess shown above, round and fertile, encouraged new life and plentiful crops.

Easter Island Figures

Oceania is the vast region of islands in the South Pacific Ocean, from Hawaii to New Zealand. Island artists have worked in materials such as wood, shells, feathers, reeds, and volcanic rock. Some of the most impressive works of Oceanic art are the giant ancestor figures of Easter Island. More than six hundred of these monumental sculptures, called *maoi,* are scattered across this tiny, remote island. They are mysterious reminders of its first inhabitants.

Stone Ancestor Figure, Easter Island,
A.D. 400–1680

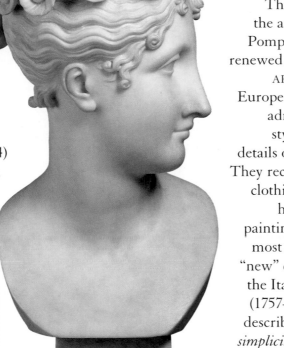

The Renaissance

The most important sculptor of the Early RENAISSANCE was Donatello (c. 1386–1466). He created figures from the Bible and legend as PORTRAITS of real people—troubled, tense, and triumphant. In the Late Renaissance, Michelangelo (1475–1564) modeled the human body—its power, energy, action, beauty, suffering, and sadness. His figures are all larger than life. His skill with marble remains unmatched.

Neoclassicism

The discovery in 1748 of the ancient Italian cities of Pompeii and Herculaneum renewed interest in CLASSICAL ART and architecture in Europe and America. Artists admired both the heroic style and the decorative details of the classical period. They recreated it in furniture, clothing, jewelry, and even hairstyles, as well as in painting and sculpture. The most noted neoclassical (or "new" classical) sculptor was the Italian Antonio Canova (1757–1822). His work was described as having *a noble simplicity and calm grandeur.*

Head of a Dancer, Marble, 1817
Antonio Canova

David (detail), Marble, 1501–03
Michelangelo

Young Girl in a Flower Hat, Terracotta, c. 1865
Auguste Rodin

Auguste Rodin (1840–1917)

The great nineteenth-century French sculptor Auguste Rodin admired Michelangelo, and was also inspired by the human form. Along with his great technical skill in creating the likeness of his subjects, Rodin searched for ways to capture their movements and expressions. Many of his most famous works—*The Kiss*, *The Thinker*, and *The Hand of God*—are familiar all over the world.

Sculpture

African Sculpture

African artists carved masks, totem figures, shields, and decorative pieces for ceremonial use. Only a few of these pieces, worked in richly colored African woods, survive. The sculptors of the Kingdom of Benin in Nigeria are famous for beautiful ivory carvings and fine bronze heads. Artists of the Kingdom of Bakuba in Congo carved a portrait of their king to praise him in life and to house his spirit ever after.

Shamba Bolongongo, 93rd King of the Bakuba, Wood, c. 1650

Untitled (Bébé Marie), early 1940s
Joseph Cornell (1903–72)

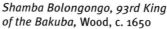

Involute, 1968
Dame Barbara Hepworth (1903–75)

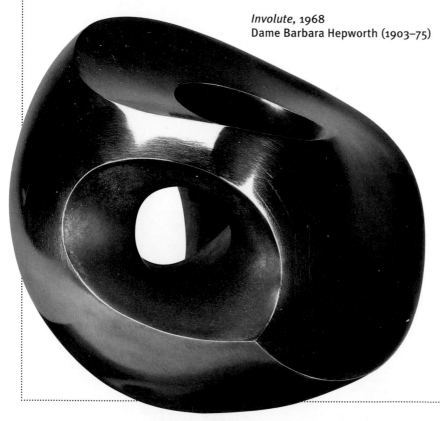

The Twentieth Century: To Cut, To Weld, To Blast?

For thousands of years sculptures were carved, chiseled, incised, gouged, and whittled. Later they were molded and cast. In the twentieth century, there was a revolution in sculpture. Artists now work with natural or man-made materials in new ways. Their work may be abstract or represent objects. They may be cut, but they can also be welded, blasted, glued, assembled in boxes, or simply arranged—in a gallery or the open air.

● *See also pages 18–19, 50–51, 62–63, 81–83, 91, 97–99*

Silk Screen

Silk screen (or serigraphy) is a method of printing in many COLORS. Inks are drawn across a screen of fine silk mesh stretched on a frame. A design is made into a STENCIL, which is attached to the screen. Then the ink is pressed through the cut-out areas with a special tool called a squeegee.

One from a set of six
Screenprints in Colors, 1979–81
Jasper Johns

Screenprint Art

Silk screen is very flexible. Cut stencils create sharp-edged designs, while a glue process gives the effect of brushstrokes to the final print. New stencil images can be prepared quickly. Prints, with many layers of brilliant color, can be created in large editions. Graphic artists and fashion designers, as well as painters and sculptors, use silk screen in interesting and unusual ways.

Shot Red Marilyn, 1964 **Andy Warhol**

Andy Warhol (1928–87)

Andy Warhol was a successful advertising artist who turned to fine art in the 1960s. He used many well-known products to create paintings and prints: soup cans, soda bottles, and soap boxes. He also used images of famous people endlessly repeated to show how fame turned them into icons (symbols) as impersonal as a soup can. In his famous New York studio, "The Factory," Warhol produced many versions of his favorite POP ART subjects, using the flat, mechanical silk-screen process. Their machine-produced feel and strong, clashing colors made them instantly recognizable. Their creator became famous in *his* turn.

● *See also pages 20–21, 42–43, 58–59, 72, 81–83, 108–109, 112–113, 124*

Stained Glass

Stained glass is shaped pieces of glass, colored with metal oxides. They are joined together with thin strips of lead to make beautiful translucent (light can pass through) panels. The technique dates from the Middle Ages, when the great cathedrals of Europe were being built (c. 1100–1400). In no other art form is light so important. It is truly "see-through" art.

Making Pictures in Glass

Stained glass has strong black outlines filled with shimmering colors. The design is prepared as a full-size CARTOON (working DRAWING) on white board. The lead lines are drawn as heavy black lines. The pieces of glass are shaped, colored, and arranged in place on the cartoon. They are then fixed with the lead and the panels mounted in the stone windows. The first large stained-glass window was put in place in the Abbey of Saint-Denis in France in 1144.

Poppy leaded glass and bronze tablelamp,
Tiffany Studios, New York,
1920

Medieval and Modern

The medieval style of making stained glass was brought back in the nineteenth century. This was done by William Morris (1834–96) and the artists of the Arts and Crafts Movement in England and by Louis Comfort Tiffany (1848–1933) in America. The elegant, decorative Tiffany lampshade, made from iridescent (rainbow-colored) glass, became a symbol of the American art nouveau style. Many great artists of the twentieth century, such as Henri Matisse and Marc Chagall, have worked in glass.

Detail of narrative panel, English Glass, 14th century

Rose Windows

In the sixteenth century, a technique for painting on glass with enamel (glasslike) COLORS was developed. Stained-glass windows became more pictorial. Windows showed stories from the Bible and history, and even flattering PORTRAITS of wealthy gift-givers. The pictures educated and entertained church-goers. However, the highest form of stained-glass art remained the magnificent rose windows of the medieval Gothic churches. These huge circular windows carry light through hundreds of small jewel-like panes into the dark interiors of vast, quiet cathedrals. The changing daylight makes the colors sparkle or fade, presenting a different spectacle every hour.

The Rose of France, Chartres Cathedral, c. 1233

● *See also pages 6–7, 14–15, 22–25, 118–119*

Stencil

A **stencil** design uses cut-out areas of a thin sheet of card or metal. COLOR is brushed or sponged over the cut-out areas onto a flat surface, such as paper, tiles, or walls. Clear, bold shapes make a strong decorative image, which can be repeated in many different colors.

Detail of stenciled fabric design

A child's kimono, with stenciled pattern, Japanese, 19th century

Stenciled Fabric

The Chinese have used stencil printing for a thousand years to make multicolored patterns on fabric. A flat-seamed Chinese coat or a Japanese kimono (robe) make a perfect surface for delicate stencil designs on cotton or silk.

Classic-style mahogany shelf clock, with painted and stenciled decoration, Hanover, Massachusetts, 1829 Benjamin Tovey

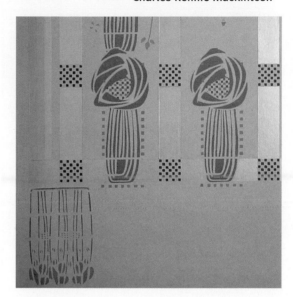

Drawing room wall stencils,
The Hill House, Helensburgh, 1903
Charles Rennie Mackintosh

Charles Rennie Mackintosh (1868–1928)

Charles Rennie Mackintosh was an architect, designer, craftsman, and artist. With his wife, Margaret Macdonald, he created what became known as the Glasgow style of art nouveau. This was based around the Glasgow School of Art in Scotland. In Mackintosh's work, curving lines, elongated (stretched) PROPORTIONS, and natural forms were put together with a cool, twentieth-century simplicity. Mackintosh worked with many different materials and techniques: STAINED GLASS, silver, painted wood, and stencil. In 1903 he designed The Hill House in Helensburgh, Scotland. It is famous for its architecture—and for the beautiful stenciled patterns that adorn its walls.

Stenciled Furniture

The northern European tradition of decorating plain wooden furniture was introduced to North America by German and Scandinavian settlers. There were forests of softwood trees in America, and the art of painting and stenciling wooden furniture, walls, and floors flourished. New designs were created by local craftsmen, as well as amateur artists. Their patterns were unique to America.

● *See also pages 35–37, 105, 116–117, 122–123*

Still Life

A **still life** painting shows objects—flowers, food, pottery, silver, cloth, even skulls—arranged on a flat surface. The separate "ingredients" may be carefully collected and arranged, or chosen at random from the everyday items in an artist's studio.

Still Life with Movement

Dutch painters of the seventeenth and eighteenth centuries created a golden age of flower painting. Jan van Huysum (1682–1749) concentrated on color and freshness. He would even wait for a flower to bloom before adding it to the COMPOSITION. His paintings were filled with movement. Leaves quiver, petals open, and bees' wings flutter.

Flowers in a Terracotta Vase, 1736–37
Jan van Huysum

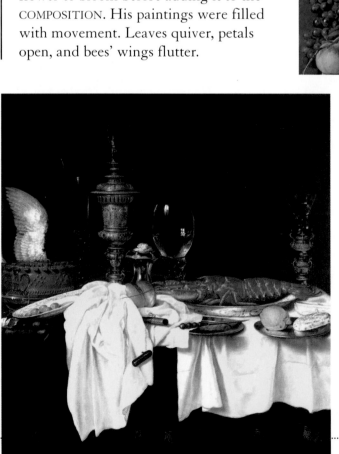

Indulgence

Dutch still-life painting was also full of symbols. The objects and their arrangement had religious meaning. Paintings showing the costly display of possessions became popular. These became known as *pronk* paintings (from the Dutch word for "show off"). They had two purposes. They displayed material wealth, but they also reminded the viewer of the sin of excess.

Still-Life with Lobster, 1650–59
Willem Claesz Heda (1594–1682)

Serenity

A vase of flowers, fruit on a dish—a still life by the French painter Henri Fantin-Latour (1836–1904) doesn't show off. Informal, calm, and domestic, Fantin-Latour's fruit and flowers would be at home on any sideboard.

The Ordinary

Gustave Caillebotte (1848–94) liked IMPRESSIONISM. He collected impressionist paintings, and shared their interest in everyday life. His own paintings, such as the fruit stand below, lovingly record the activities of the quiet quarter of Paris where he lived.

Still Life with Roses, Fruit, and a Glass of Wine,
1872 Henri Fantin-Latour

Fruit Displayed on a Stand, c. 1880 Gustave Caillebotte

A New Way of Looking ...

Artists in the twentieth century experimented with reality in painting, flattening PERSPECTIVE and giving new forms to familiar objects. The Spanish painter Juan Gris (1887–1927) gave his breakfast table a special cubist treatment, making us think about the shapes of cups, saucers, and the morning paper.

Breakfast, 1914 Juan Gris

● *See also pages 32–33, 46–47, 54–55, 68–71, 73, 114–115, 120–121*

Street Art

Street art is public art, created for public spaces. Its aim is attention-seeking; its purpose is to convey information. It sells, persuades, warns, and entertains. Street art may appear in many forms—posters, banners, sculpture, advertisements, neon signs, even graffiti.

Advertising Art

The most popular form of street art today is advertising art. But it isn't new. It started over five thousand years ago in Babylon, where the most memorable, funny, or best-designed shop sign might catch a customer's eye and bring more trade. The invention of the printing press in the fifteenth century brought an explosion of ephemeral (or throw-away) street art in the form of handbills and posters. These had text and engraved illustrations, and the day's news or events reached a huge audience. By the nineteenth century, full-color posters were a popular art form. Artists such as Henri de Toulouse-Lautrec and Pablo Picasso provided images for advertising posters. "Brand characters" became associated with favorite products. The poster advertising an international exhibition of advertising in 1920 includes a gallery of well-known images, including the Kodak Girl and the first Michelin Man!

Underground to Wood Lane: International Advertising Exhibition at The White City, 1920 Frederick Charles Herrick

Propaganda Art

Well-designed graphic images with strong clear messages have played an important part in the history of the last century. Modern printing methods can reproduce an image in full color many thousands of times. The message—to vote for a candidate, join an organization, or support a cause—will quickly reach many people. Some images become icons (symbols) of a time and place. They are easily recognized by anyone who sees them—the pointing finger of Uncle Sam on a 1917 army recruiting poster, the face of the 1960s revolutionary Che Guevara, the stylized CALLIGRAPHY of the Polish trade union Solidarity in the 1980s.

I Want You For U.S. Army, 1917
James Montgomery Flagg

Individual Art: Graffiti

Graffiti—covering buildings, bridges, or trains with "tags" (the artists' names or logos) and paintings —is a modern art form. It started in inner-city areas in the 1970s. To some, this spray-can art by agile young artists brightens drab urban spaces. To others it is vandalism. A few painters used graffiti styles in their work, including the American Jean-Michel Basquiat (1960–1988).

Apex, 1986 Jean-Michel Basquiat

● *See also pages 14–15, 28–31, 34, 60–61, 66–67, 81–83, 105*

Surrealism

With **surrealism** artists tried to release the creative power of the subconscious mind. Beginning in the 1920s, surrealist writers and artists created images in which the familiar meets the fantastic in a new, dreamlike world. They seem to be beyond "real" (or super-real).

Object (Luncheon in Fur), 1936 Meret Oppenheim (1913–85)

Portrait, 1935 René Magritte

René Magritte (1898–1967)

The Belgian artist René Magritte designed wallpaper and advertising posters. His paintings display an interest in everyday life. But it is an ordinary world in which very strange things happen. Loaves of bread fly, fish run on human legs, and office workers leave home without their faces. The "stories" of his paintings are always mysterious, unsettling, and very witty. Magritte warns us that nothing is as it seems. Even beautifully painted objects cannot be trusted. The table precisely laid for lunch has secrets to reveal. His imagery and wit made Magritte one of the most popular surrealist painters.

Salvador Dalí (1904–89)

The most famous of all the surrealists was the extraordinary Spanish painter Salvador Dalí. His life was often as strange as the images that appeared in his work. He called his paintings *"hand-painted dream photographs"* and filled them with odd, dreamlike details painted with great care. They were also full of tricks. Drawers open out of a human figure or a desert LANDSCAPE transforms itself into a haunted, staring face.

Paranoic Face, 1935 Salvador Dalí

● *See also pages 94–96*

Symmetry

Symmetry is the arrangement of parts of a picture so that its halves are in BALANCE—equal in size and PROPORTION on either side of an imaginary central line. **Symmetry** can be pleasing and natural to our eyes. Many things in nature are symmetrical.

Asymmetry: Being Unbalanced

Asymmetry occurs when pictures are arranged to be unbalanced. It catches our eye by creating tension or appearing unnatural or disturbing. Japanese artists used asymmetrical COMPOSITIONS to give extra power to their images. This was one of the many aspects of Japanese art that influenced European artists from the nineteenth century onward.

Travellers on the Tokaido Road, 1834–35
Utagawa Kuniyoshi (1798–1861)

Geometry: Balance and Precision

Draw a line vertically (up and down) through the middle of a face. The two sides are not mirror images of each other. Small differences make our faces imperfect, and more interesting. Only precise geometrical shapes—squares, circles, and the like—are perfectly symmetrical. Josef Albers (1888–1976) spent twenty years studying squares. Placing squares of similar COLOR inside one another, he created cool, balanced images.

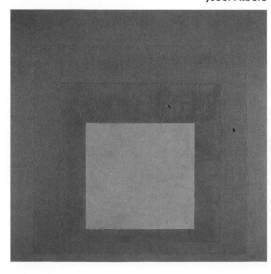

Study for Homage to the Square: Contralto, 1957
Josef Albers

● *See also pages 6–7, 10–11, 26–27, 72, 74–75, 92–93, 124*

Tapestry

Tapestry is a kind of heavy cloth, handwoven on a loom to create a multicolored picture. Horizontal threads (weft) of wool or silk are woven tightly through vertical threads (warp) of linen, giving a smooth, unbroken surface.

Woven Pictures

The ancient art of tapestry was at its height in medieval Europe. The rooms and halls of castles, churches, and even royal palaces were large, high-ceilinged, and chilly. They needed to be made warm and cheerful during the winter. Huge tapestries designed by famous painters provided warmth and entertainment. They were the wallpaper and the television of the Middle Ages—featuring stories from classical mythology and the Bible, tales of courtly love, and crowded hunting and battle scenes.

The Woodpecker Tapestry, woven at Morris Merton Abbey Workshops, c. 1885 William Morris

Boar and Bear Hunt, Devonshire Hunting Tapestry, 1425–50

● *See also pages 14–15, 52–53, 122–123*

Theme

La Primavera (The Spring), c. 1478
Sandro Botticelli

Works of art can tell a story or express an idea. That story or idea is the **theme**. Artists often use stories to illustrate a proverb or teach a lesson. By understanding the themes behind the work, we can discover a great deal about the customs and beliefs of people who lived long ago.

Nymphs and Goddesses

The Florentine painter Sandro Botticelli (c. 1444–1510) filled his canvases with imagination and meaning. His early works used characters, ideas, and symbols from Roman mythology. One theme of *La Primavera* is the spring and birth. At the far right are the West Wind and a pregnant nymph. Their daughter was Flora, the goddess of spring and flowering plants. She is shown casting a carpet of flowers. At the center is Venus, the goddess of love. Above her is Cupid, shooting one of his arrows toward the dancing figures of Three Graces. At the far left is Mercury, the messenger of the gods, fanning away clouds. Everything in this beautiful picture has a symbolic meaning. Yet we can also enjoy it for its artistry of line and COLOR.

A Village Festival in Honour of St. Hubert and St. Anthony, undated
Pieter Brueghel II (1564–1638)

Early Social History

In the 1500s and 1600s, the Brueghels, the great Flemish family of painters, painted scenes both real and imaginary. Using a high viewpoint and wide-angle "stage," they celebrated village life in northern Europe—the changing seasons, festivals, and the hard work of ordinary people. The theme of the painting at left is enjoyment: stalls and shows, rides, children's games, food and drink—a happy break from daily cares.

 ● *See also pages 10–11, 14–15, 26–27, 50–55, 66–71, 74–79, 92–96, 98–101, 106–107, 110–115, 117, 120–121, 124*

Storytelling 19th-Century Style

The Derby Day by Sir William Powell Frith (1819–1909) is also about enjoyment—a day at the races. But its real theme is very different. Here are all classes, enjoying the same sporting event, yet they are separated by their place in English Victorian society. For the middle classes the race is a chance to see and be seen. The laborers are enjoying a holiday from work, like Brueghel's Flemish villagers. Between them are the racing men, making a professional visit.

The Derby Day, 1856–58 **William Powell Frith**

Watercolor

Watercolor is a painting technique using pigments (coloring powder) diluted (thinned) with water to create transparent washes. The quick-drying paint is applied with soft hair brushes on rough-textured paper. The white of the paper brings light through the thin layers of paint.

Flowers and Cats

Elizabeth Blackadder (b. 1931) handles watercolor with wonderful freshness. Her series of paintings of huge-petalled flowers and casual cats recall the great age of eighteenth-century botanical (plant) paintings.

Poppies and Black Cat, 1986 Elizabeth Blackadder

The Blue Boat, 1892 Winslow Homer

Catching the Scene

The American artist Winslow Homer (1836–1910) described his approach to painting: *"When I have selected the thing carefully, I paint it exactly as it appears."* His great skill made it look easy. He created atmosphere with swift strokes of color. *The Blue Boat* moves slowly through the water—still looking fresh and wet more than a century after it was painted.

Strong, Bright Color

Watercolor was used on
papyrus (a paperlike
material) by the ancient
Egyptians and on
handmade rice paper
by Chinese artists.
The technique spread
throughout the world.
Indian painters painted
gods and heroes in
glowing colors to show
their strength and power.
This is Vishnu, painted
in flat primary COLORS,
his skin a magnificent
deep blue.

Vishnu in the Dwarf Incarnation of Vamana,
Kalighat (Calcutta), c. 1885

● *See also pages 22–25, 56–57, 94–96, 100–101*

Weaving

Weaving is an ancient technique of making textiles (cloth) from threads of cotton, wool, silk, or linen. Working on a machine called a loom, the weaver works free threads (weft) in and out of fixed threads (warp) with a shuttle (thread-holder).

Weft and Warp

In weaving, the pattern is part of the fabric itself. The shapes and COLORS are carefully planned by the weaver. They are built up as the horizontal weft threads are woven through the vertical warp threads. The weft is left loose for an "open weave," or pressed tightly after each row for a smoother texture.

The Richness of Silk

Ikat weaving produces soft, luxurious fabrics in shimmering colors, especially when woven from silk threads. The pattern is made in the long warp threads, which are dyed in sections before they are fixed to the loom. Ikats come from Asia, South America, and Africa. Ikat silks are highly prized: rich robes became the traditional costumes for Japanese theater; and fine saris (draped clothing) from India were once used as money.

Ikat, Mashra Fabric in cotton and silk, four lengths,
Tamil Nadu, mid-19th century

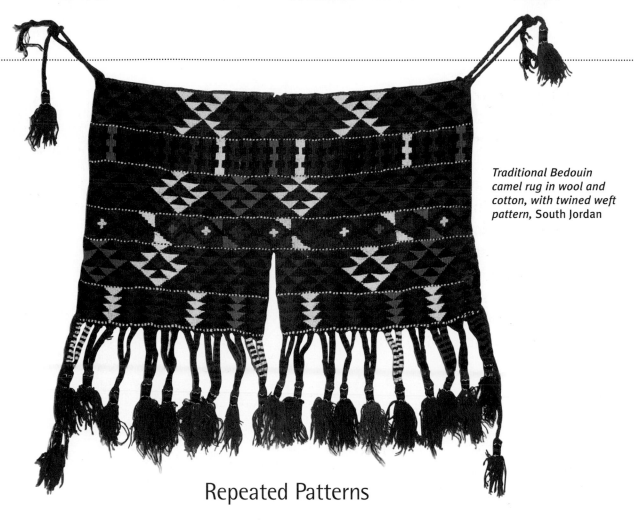

Traditional Bedouin camel rug in wool and cotton, with twined weft pattern, South Jordan

Repeated Patterns

Woven rugs, hangings, and pictorial bedspreads have been a favorite—and practical—art form in Scandinavia since the Middle Ages. Pictorial folk bedspreads show stories from the Bible. But the Norwegians turned away from a naturalistic style toward a flat, decorative style. Norwegian artists also weave strong woolen rugs in colorful geometric patterns. Similar patterns are found in Native American Navajo blankets from the American southwest, and Bedouin camel rugs from the Middle East.

Straw, Reeds, and Feathers

Some kinds of weaving can be done without a loom. In many parts of the world, straw, reeds, and dried grasses are handwoven to make bags, baskets, and mats. Dried fibers, dyed with natural colors, are braided, twisted, or woven in complicated designs of great delicacy. Maori artists of New Zealand add feathers and other materials to give further beauty to their work.

Maori Patterned Baskets, New Zealand, 20th century

● *See also pages 35–37, 64–65, 72, 88–90, 108–109, 117*

oodcut

Woodcuts are made by a RELIEF technique of printing. First the design is drawn onto wood. Areas that will appear white are cut or gouged away. The raised lines are inked and pressed against paper, leaving a copy of the design.

Japanese Woodblock Prints

In eighteenth-century Japan artists created multicolored woodblock prints of city life. Festivals, journeys, poems, pretty ladies, and popular actors of the Kabuki theater were all celebrated in ukiyo-e ("pictures of the floating world"). Printed in thousands, they were enjoyed like magazines today.

The Schoolmaster, 1510 Albrecht Dürer

Engraving on Wood

For wood ENGRAVING, fine tools called burins are used to cut into small blocks of hardwood. The English wood engraver Thomas Bewick (1753–1828) made hundreds of careful studies of animals for his famous book *A General History of Quadrupeds.*

The Leicestershire Improved Breed, from *A General History of Quadrupeds,* 1788 Thomas Bewick

Geisha wiping her Face, Modern Beauties,
Oban-size woodblock print, late 1820s
Utagawa Kunisada

● *See also pages 42–43, 97, 116*

Index

A

Abstract art 6-7, 8, 9, 12, 28, 32, 82
Action painting 6, 8-9, 13
Adams, Ansel 78
Advertising art 112
African carving 32, 33, 60, 104
Aho, Kaarina 90
Albers, Josef 116
Altamira 91
American decorative art 36
American naturalists 95
Andrea del Sarto 10
Appel, Karel 9
Aquatint 42, 43
Arab art *see* Islamic art
Art nouveau 37, 109
Arts and Crafts Movement 107
Assemblage 21
Asymmetry 37, 116
Aztec 64, 67

B

Bakuba 104
Balance 10-11, 12, 26, 62
Basquiat, Jean-Michel 113
Bayer, Herbert 79
Bedouin 123
Bellamy, John 17
Benin 104
Benninck, Simon 53
Bewick, Thomas 124
Bierstadt, Albert 57
Blackadder, Elizabeth 120
Blake, Peter 82
Bonnard, Pierre 23
Book of Kells 52
Books of Hours 53
Botticelli, Sandro 118

Brady, Mathew 77
Braque, Georges 32, 33
Brown, Mary 36
Brueghel, Pieter II 118
Brunelleschi, Filippo 74

C

Caillebotte, Gustave 111
Calder, Alexander 62, 63
Calligraphy 12-13, 52, 113
Cameron, Julia Margaret 76
Canova, Antonio 103
Caravaggio 68
Carpaccio, Vittore 99
Cartier-Bresson, Henri 79
Cartoon 14-15, 106
Carving 16-17, 32, 33, 60, 97, 98, 104
Cassatt, Mary 43, 71
Cave art 91
Cézanne, Paul 27, 32, 86
Chagall, Marc 59, 107
Chevreul, Michel Eugène 22
Chiaroscuro 43, 69
Chinese 12, 38, 60, 88, 108, 121
Christo 31
Classical art 18-19
Collage 20-1, 56
Cologne School 106
Colonial America 109
Color 22-5, 26, 33, 35, 38, 44, 47, 48, 54, 56, 58, 68, 72, 73, 80, 91, 96, 99, 100, 105, 107, 108, 116, 118, 121, 122
Composition 24, 26-7, 39, 48, 57, 58, 80, 85, 99, 110, 116
Computer art 28-9
Conceptual art 30-1
Constable, John 41, 57, 100

Cornell, Joseph 104
Corot, Jean-Baptiste-Camille 56
Courbet, Gustave 94
Cubism 6, 20, 21, 27, 32-3, 111

D

Dada 20, 21, 30, 32, 34
Dalí, Salvador 115
Daumier, Honoré 58
de Kooning, Willem 9
Decorative arts 6, 35-7
Decorative masks 60
Degas, Edgar 73
Delacroix, Eugène 100
Donatello 46, 48, 98, 103
Dong Qichang 12
Dove, Arthur G. 20
Drawing 14, 20, 38-9, 43, 47, 48, 56, 73, 87, 95, 106
Drypoint 42, 43
Duchamp, Marcel 21, 34
Dürer, Albrecht 42, 124
Castel Durrante 89

E

Eakins, Thomas 95
Earth art 40-1
Easter Island 102
Egyptians 35, 66, 121
Engraving 42-3, 56, 68, 69, 124
Ephemera 112
Etching 42, 43
Expressionism 8, 9, 44-5

F

Fantin-Latour, Henri 111
Fauvism 33, 46-7
Fenton, Roger 77
Flagg, James Montgomery 113

Foreshortening 48-9, 51
Fresco 10, 14, 27, 48, 49, 50-1, 66, 93, 99
Friedrich, Caspar David 101
Frith, Sir William Powell 119

Gainsborough, Thomas 70
Gauguin, Paul 86, 87
Geometry 28, 89
Ghiberti, Lorenzo 97
Gibbons, Grinling 16, 17
Gillray, James 15
Glasgow School of Art 109
Gogh, Vincent van 11, 44, 46, 86, 87
Goldsworthy, Andy 40
Gouache 59
Gould, Peter 28
Goya, Francisco de 84
Graffiti 113
El Greco 44
Greeks 18, 19, 61, 98
Gris, Juan 111
Grünewald, Mathis 44

Hamilton, Richard 82
Heda, Willem Claesz 110
Hepworth, Barbara 104
Herrick, Frederick Charles 112
Hogarth, William 15
Homer, Winslow 120
Hooch, Pieter de 75
Hopi Indians 60
Huysum, Jan van 110

Ikat weaving 122
Illumination 12, 52-3
Impasto 71
Impressionism 23, 54-5, 71, 80, 111
Indians 121
Intaglio Printing 42

Inuit 17
Islamic art 12, 37, 89

Japanese 12, 24, 38, 58, 61, 88, 108, 116, 122, 124
Johns, Jasper 81, 82, 105
Johnston, Edward 12

Kaendler, J.J. 89
Kandinsky, Wassily 6, 7
Killiktee, Shorty 17
Kinetic art 62, 63
Klee, Paul 13
Kline, Franz 9
Kokoschka, Oskar 44, 45
Kosuth, Joseph 30
Kunisada, Utagawa 61, 124
Kuniyoshi, Utagawa 116

Lalique, René 37
Landscape 7, 31, 38, 40, 43, 47, 56-7, 70, 78, 96, 100, 101
Lascaux 91
Lasseter, John 29
Leach, Bernard 90
Léger, Fernand 65
Leonardo da Vinci 14, 39, 92
Lichtenstein, Roy 82, 83
Limbourg, Pol de 53
Linares, Leonardo 61
Lincoln, Abraham 77
Line engraving 42
Lippi, Filippo 98
Lithography 58-9
Long, Richard 41

Macdonald, Margaret 109
Mackintosh, Charles Rennie 37, 109
Magritte, René 114

Majolica 89
Manet, Edouard 54
Mantegna, Andrea 48, 49
Maori 123
Masquerade 60-1
Master of the Life of the Virgin 56
Matisse, Henri 46, 47, 107
Meusnier, Georges 55
Mexico 61, 64, 67
Mezzotint 42
Michelangelo 50-1, 97, 103
Mixtec-Aztec 64
Mobile 62-3
Mondrian, Piet 7
Monet, Claude 55
Moore, Henry 38
Morris, William 107, 117
Mosaic 59, 64-5
Mucha, Alphonse 112
Munch, Edvard 44, 45
Mural 66-7

Native Americans 60, 123
Naturalism 94-6
Navajo 123
Neoclassicism 103
New York 7, 9, 34, 72
North American Indians 60, 123

Objets trouvés 21
Oil painting 22, 59, 68-71
O'Keefe, Georgia 25
Oldenburg, Claes 83
Op art 72
Oppenheim, Meret 114

Pacific Islands 60, 102
Palmer, Samuel 100
Paolozzi, Eduardo 82
Papier-mâché 60, 61
Parthenon 19

Pastel 22, 73
Patchwork 36
Perspective 11, 26, 32, 38, 39, 48, 74-5, 99, 111
Peru 35
Peto, John Frederick 94
Phidias 19
Photography 76-9, 95
Photolithography 81
Picasso, Pablo 32, 33, 90, 112
Picturesque 101
Piero della Francesca 26, 27
Pigments 50, 68, 73, 96, 120
Pissarro, Camille 54
Pointillism 80
Pollock, Jackson 8, 9
Pop art 30, 81-83
Portrait 19, 68, 70, 84-5, 99, 103, 107
Post-Impressionism 86-7
Posters 112
Pottery 18, 21, 33, 35, 88-90
Prehistoric art 91, 102
Printing 42, 43, 112, 113
Pronk paintings 110
Propaganda art 113
Proportion 39, 92-3, 109, 116

Raphael 14, 99
Rauschenberg, Robert 21
Ravenna 65
Realism 94-6
Redon, Odilon 73
Relief 16, 19, 42, 97, 98, 124
Rembrandt van Rijn 43, 69, 84
Renaissance 10, 27, 39, 46, 50, 56, 98-9, 103
Renoir, Pierre-Auguste 71
Repton, Humphrey 42
Rietveld, Gerrit 6

Riley, Bridget 72
Rivera, Diego 67
Rodin, Auguste 103
Romans 12, 19, 64, 97, 98
Romanticism 41, 56, 100-1
Rothko, Mark 25
Rowlandson, Thomas 15
Rubens, Sir Peter Paul 68, 69, 70

Sardonyx cameo 97
Sargent, John Singer 85
Satire 15
Scandinavia 123
Scarfe, Gerald 15
School of Herefordshire 97
Schwitters, Kurt 20
Sculpture 18, 21, 33, 34, 38, 46, 62, 63, 72, 82, 83, 90, 91, 97, 102-4
Senefelder, Aloys 58
Seurat, Georges-Pierre 80
Silk screen 21, 81, 105
Sistine Chapel 14, 50-1
Smithson, Robert 40
Social comment 15
Stabiles 63
Stained glass 14, 59, 106-7, 109
Steadman, Ralph 15
Stencil 36, 105, 108-9
de Stijl 6
Still life 47, 68, 110-11
Strand, Paul 78
Street art 112-13
Surrealism 114-15
Symbols 81, 83, 113, 118
Symmetry 116

Talbot, William Henry Fox 76
Tamil Nadu 122

Tapestry 14, 59, 68, 117
Tempera 96
Theater 59, 61
Theme 32, 55, 59, 80, 118-19
Tiffany, Louis Comfort 107
Tinguely, Jean 62
Tinware 36
Titian (Tiziano Vecelli) 22
Toby, Mark 13
Toulouse-Lautrec, Henri de 58, 112
Tovey, Benjamin 109
Trompe l'oeil 49, 66, 94
Turner, J.M.W. 41, 101
Tzara, Tristan 34

Uccello, Paolo 74

Vasarely, Victor 72
Vasari, Georgio 39, 98
Vermeer, Jan 11, 75
Veronese, Paolo 93
Vitruvius 92
Vlaminck, Maurice de 46

Walpole, Horace 16
Warhol, Andy 81, 82, 105
Watercolor 24, 59, 73, 120-1
Weaving 122-3
Weston, Brett 78
Weston, Edward 78
Whistler, James Abbot McNeil 24
Woodcut 42, 58, 124
Wordsworth, William 100
Wyeth, Andrew 96

Zhang Zongchang 38

Acknowledgments

The Author and Publisher wish to thank the following museums and agencies for permission to reproduce copyright material:

The V & A Picture Library, London for pages 6 right, 12 left (Photo: Ian Thomas), 14 below (Royal Loan), 15 above and below left, 16 above and below, 37, above right, 42 above, 53 below left and right, 58 right, 61 above, 76 above and below, 77 below, 79 below, 88 above right, left, and below right, 89 above left, above right, center and below right, 90 above and below right, 97 below right, 100 above right, 101 above right, 103 above, 106, 108 above and below, 112, 116 above, 117 below, 121, 122, and 124 below left (All images Courtesy of the Trustees of the V & A) ; **INDEX, Firenze** for half-title detail and page 119 above (Firenze, Uffizi/Photo: INDEX ~ Perugi), pages 10 (Roma, Galleria Spada/Photo: Archivo Fotografico Soprintendenza BAS, Roma), 22 above (Napoli, Capodimonte/Photo: Pedicini), 26~27 above (Arezzo, San Francisco/Photo: INDEX ~Pizzi), 48 (Milano, Brera/Photo: Ag. Ricciarini, Milano), 49 (Palazzo Ducale, Mantua/Photo: Giovetti), 50~51 (Vaticano, Cappella Sistina/Photo: Archivo Fotografico Musei Vaticani/Brachetti, Zigrossi), 65 above (Ravenna, San Appollinare Nuovo/Photo: Ag. Ricciarini, Milano), 65 center (Ravenna, Mausoleo di Galla Placida/Photo: Ghigo Roli), 91 below (Spagna, Grotta di Altamira/Photo:Ag. Ricciarni, Milano), 92 below left, 92~93, and 93 below right (Venezia Accademia /Photo: Bohm), 97 left (Firenze Battistero/Photo: INDEX ~ Tosi), 98 (Firenze, Bargello/Photo: Vasari), and 103 (Firenze, Accademia/Photo: INDEX ~ Tosi); **The Museum of Modern Art, New York** for pages 7 (MONDRIAN, Piet. *Broadway Boogie Woogie.* 1942~43. Oil on canvas, 50 x 50" [127 x 127 cm]. The Museum of Modern Art, New York. Given anonymously, Photograph © 2000 The Museum of Modern Art, New York.), 13 right (TOBEY, Mark. *Edge of August.* 1953. Casein on composition board, 48 x 28" [121.9 x 71.1 cm]. The Museum of Modern Art, New York. Purchase. Photograph © 2000 The Museum of Modern Art, New York), 20 above (DOVE, Arthur G. *Grandmother.* 1925. Collage of shingles, needlepoint, page from the Concordance, pressed flowers, and ferns, mounted on cloth-covered wood, 20 x 21 1/4" [50.8 x 54 cm]. The Museum of Modern Art, New York. Gift of Philip L. Goodwin [by exchange]. Photograph © 2000 The Museum of Modern Art, New York), 30 (KOSUTH, Joseph. *One and Three Chairs.* 1965. Wooden folding chair, photographic copy of a chair, and photographic enlargement of a dictionary definition of a chair; chair 32 3/8 x 14 7/8 x 20 7/8' [82 x 37.8 x 53 cm]; photo panel, 36 x 24 1/8" [91.5 x 61.1 cm]; text panel, 24 x 24 1/8" [61 x 61.3 cm]. The Museum of Modern Art, New York. Larry Aldrich Foundation Fund. Photograph © 2000 The Museum of modern art, New York), 32 left (BRAQUE, Georges. *Guitar.* Summer 1913. Gesso, pasted papers, charcoal, pencil and gouache on canvas, 39 1/4 x 25 5/8" [99.7 x 65.1 cm]. The Museum of Modern Art, New York. Acquired through the Lillie P. Bliss Bequest. Photograph © 2000 The Museum of Modern Art, New York), 33 above (PICASSO, Pablo. *Girl Before a Mirror.* Boisgeloup, March 1932. Oil on canvas, 64 x 51 1/4" [162.3 x 130.2 cm]. The Museum of Modern Art, New York. Gift of Mrs. Simon Guggenheim. Photograph © 2000 The Museum of Modern Art, New York. © Succession Picasso/DACS 2000), 44 (VAN GOGH, Vincent. *The Starry Night.* 1889. Oil on canvas, 29 x 36 1/4" [73.7 x 92.1 cm]. The Museum of Modern Art, New York. Acquired through the Lillie P. Bliss Bequest. Photograph© 2000 The Museum of Modern Art, New York), 58 left (TOULOUSE-LAUTREC, Henri de. *Reine de Joie.* 1892. Lithograph, printed in color, composition: [irregular] 53 7/8 x 36 3/4" [136.8 x 93.3 cm]. The Museum of Modern Art, New York. Gift of Mr. and Mrs. Richard Rodgers. Photograph © 2000 The Museum of Modern Art, New York), 62 above (CALDER, Alexander. *Lobster Trap and Fish Tail.* 1939. Hanging mobile: painted steel wire and sheet aluminum, about 8' 6" h. x 9' 6" diameter [260 x 290 cm]. The Museum of Modern Art, New York. Commissioned by the Advisory Committee for the stairwell of the museum. Photograph © 2000 The Museum of Modern Art, New York), 73 above (REDON, Odilon. *Vase of Flowers.* 1914. Pastel on paper, 28 3/4 x 21 1/8" [73 x 53.7 cm]. The Museum of Modern art, New York. The William S. Paley Collection. Photograph © 2000 The Museum of Modern Art, New York), 83 above (OLDENBURG, Claes. *Two Cheeseburgers with Everything (Dual Hamburgers).* 1962. Burlap soaked in plaster, painted with enamel, 7 x 14 3/4 x 8 5/8" [17.8 x 37.5 x 21.6 cm]. The Museum of Modern Art, New York. Philip Johnson Fund. Photograph © 2000 The Museum of Modern Art, New York), 86 below (CEZANNE, Paul. *Still Life with Ginger Jar, Sugar Bowl, and Oranges.* 1902~06. Oil on canvas, 23 7/8 x 28 7/8" [60.6 x 73.3 cm]. The Museum of Modern Art, New York. Lillie P. Bliss Collection. Photograph © 2000 The Museum of Modern Art, New York), 104 above right (CORNELL, Joseph. *Untitled (Bebe Marie).* early 1940s. Papered and painted wood box, with painted corrugated cardboard floor, containing doll in cloth dress and straw hat with cloth flowers, dried flowers, and twigs, flecked with paint. 23 1/2 x 12 3/8 x 5 1/4" [59.7 x 31.5 x 13.3 cm]. The Museum of Modern Art, New York. Acquired through the Lillie P. Bliss Bequest. Photograph © 2000 The Museum of Modern Art, New York), 111 below right (GRIS, Juan. *Breakfast.* 1914. Cut-and-pasted paper, crayon, and oil over canvas, 31 7/8 x 23 1/2" [80.9 x 59.7 cm]. The Museum of Modern Art, New York. Acquired through the Lillie P. Bliss Bequest. Photograph © 2000 The Museum of Modern Art, New York), 114 above (OPPENHEIM, Meret. *Object (Le Dejeuner en Fourrure).* 1936. Fur-covered cup, saucer, and spoon; cup 4 3/8" [10.9 cm] diameter; saucer, 9 3/8 [23.7 cm] diameter; spoon 8"[20.2 cm] long; overall height 2 7/8" [7.3 cm]. The Museum of Modern Art, New York. Purchase. Photograph © 2000 The Museum of Modern Art, New York), and 114 below (MAGRITTE, Rene. *Portrait (Le Portrait).* 1935. Oil on canvas, 28 7/8 x 19 7/8" [73.3 x 50.2 cm]. The Museum of Modern Art, New York. Gift of Kay Sage Tanguy. Photograph © 2000 The Museum of Modern Art, New York); **The National Gallery, London** for pages 11, 14 above, 26 below, 56 below, 56~57 above, 57 above right, 68, 70, 74, 80, 84 above and below, 94 below, 98 below, and 110 above and below (All works Reproduced by Courtesy of the Trustees, The National Gallery, London.); **The British Museum, London** for pages 15 below right, 18 above and below, 19 above, center, and below, 35 above and below. 37 below left, 60 left, 61 below, 64 below, 66, 97 above, 102 below, 104 above left, 123 above and below, and cover left (All works © Copyright The British Museum); **The British Library, London** for page 52 below left (MS 42130 f173b/B438 By Permission of the British Library); **Art Gallery of Ontario, Toronto** for page 17 below (Killiktie, Shorty (m) Lake Harbour, 1949-. Greenstone and ivory, 24.5 x 14.3 x 14.4 cm. Gift of the Klamer Family, 1978. Reproduced by Permission of the West Baffin Eskimo Co-operative ltd.); **The Bibliotheque Nationale, Paris** for page 22 below; **The Minneapolis Institute of Arts** for page 23; **Tate Gallery, London** for pages 24 above (Bequeathed by W.C. Alexander, 1932), 24 below, 54 above, 82 left (© Eduardo Paolozzi 2000. All Rights Reserved, DACS), and 119 below (All images © Tate Gallery, London 1999); **The Phillips Collection, Washington, D.C.** for page 25; **Art Resource, New York** for page 21 (© Untitled Press, Inc./VAGA, NY/DACS, London 2000 ~ Photo: ESM-Ed Meneely/Art Resource, NY), and 67 (Reproduced by permission of The Ministry of Public Education, Mexico City ~ Photo: Bob Schalkwijk/Art Resource, NY); **Oxford Scientific Films** for page 28 (Photo: © Art Matrix); **© Disney Enterprises Inc.** for page 29 (Photo: Courtesy The Kobal Collection); **Philadelphia Museum of Art** for pages 34 (The Louise and Walter Arensberg Collection/© Succession Marcel Duchamp /ADAGP, Paris and DACS, London 2000, Photo: Graydon Wood, 1994), and 36 below (Coffeepot: Gift of Mrs. William D, Frishmuth/Tea Caddy: Purchase, Special Museum Fund; **Christies Images, London** for page 6 left (© ADAGP, Paris and DACS, London 2000, 8~9 below (© ARS, NY and DACS, London 2000), 9 above (© DACS, 2000), 12 right, 13 left (© DACS, 2000), 17 above, 20 below (© DACS, London 2000), 25 above right (© ARS, NY and DACS, London 2000), 31 (© DACS, London 2000), 32 above right (© Succession Picasso/DACS 2000), 33 below (© DACS, London 2000), 36 above, 38 above, 38 below (Reproduced by Permission of The Henry Moore Foundation), 41 (Courtesy The Antony d'Offay Gallery), 45 above (© Munch Museum/Munch-Ellingsen Group, BONO, Oslo, DACS, London 2000), 45 below (© DACS 2000), 46 (© ADAGP, Paris and DACS, London 2000), 54 below, 55 above, 57 below, 59 (© ADAGP, Paris and DACS, London 2000), 60 above and center, 63 (©ADAGP, Paris and DACS, London 2000), 71 above and below, 72 above (© ADAGP, Paris and DACS, London 2000), 72 below (© Bridget Riley), 78 above and below (The Association of Photographers), 79 above (© DACS 2000), 81 above (© Licensed by The Andy Warhol Foundation for the Visual Arts, Inc./DACS, London 2000. Trademarks Licensed by Campbell Soup Company. All Rights Reserved.), 81 below (© Jasper Johns/VAGA,NY /DACS, London 2000), 82 above (© Peter Blake 2000. All Rights Reserved, DACS), 83 below (© The Estate of Roy Lichtenstein/DACS 2000), 87 (© The Bridgeman Art Library 2000), 90 below left (© Succession Picasso /DACS 2000), 94 above, 95, 100 below left, 104 below left (Courtesy , Sir Allen Bowness, Hepworth Estate), 105 above (© DACS, London 2000), 105 below (© The Andy Warhol Foundation for the Visual Arts, Inc./ARS, NY and DACS, London 2000/TM2000 Estate of Marilyn Monroe by CMG Worldwide Inc.), 107 below, 109 left, 111 above right, 113 (© ADAGP, Paris and DACS, London 2000), 115 (© Salvador Dalí-Foundation Gala-Salvador Dalí), and 116 below (© DACS 2000) (All Photos © Christies Images Ltd); **Julian Bicknell** for pages 37 center and 107 right; **The Royal Collection © 2000 Her Majesty Queen Elizabeth II** for page 39; **Scottish National Gallery of Modern Art** for pages 40~41 below (Andy Goldsworthy. *Crack Line Through Leaves.* Courtesy, the Artist); **The Metropolitan Museum of Art, New York** for pages 43 below (Gift of Paul J. Sachs, (16.2.9)/Photo: (© 1991 Metropolitan Museum of Art), 73 below (Bequest of Mrs. H. O.Havemeyer, 1929. The H.O. Havemeyer Collection (29.100.38)/Photograph (© 1987 The Metropolitan Museum of Art), and cover right (Catherine Lorillard Wolfe Fund, 1963. (63.85)/Photograph (© 1991 The Metropolitan Museum of Art); **Rijksmuseum, Amsterdam** for page 43 above; **National Gallery of Art, Washington** for page 47 (Collection of Mr.and Mrs. Paul Mellon, © Board of Trustees National Gallery of Art, Washington/Photo: Richard Carafelli (© Succession H. Matisse/DACS 2000; **The Bridgeman Art Library** for pages 52 above (The Board of Trinity College, Dublin, Ireland/BAL), 53 above (Musee Conde, Chantilly/Giraudon/BAL), 101 below (Kunsthalle, Hamburg, Germany/BAL), and 113 above (Imperial War Museum, London, UK/BAL); **Museum of Fine Arts, Boston** for pages 55 below (*Water Lilies I*, 1905: Claude Monet, French [1840~1926]. Oil on Canvas; unframed 89.5 x 100.3 cm [35 3/16 x 39 1/2 in.]. Gift of Edward Jackson Holmes, 39.804), 69 above (*Head of Cyrus Brought to Queen Tomyris,* about 1622~23; Peter Paul Rubens, Flemish [1577~1640]. Oil on canvas ; unframed 205 x 361 cm [80 11/16 x 142 1/8 in.] Juliana Cheney Edwards Collection, 41.40.), 85 above (*The Daughters of Edward Darley Boit,* 1882: John Singer Sargent, American [1836~1925]. Oil on canvas; Overall 221.9 x 222.6 cm [87 3/8 x 87 5/8 in.]. Gift of Mary Louisa Boit, Julia Overing Boit, Jane Hubbard Boit, and Florence D. Boit in memory of their father, Edward Darley Boit, 19.124), 86 above (*Madame Cezanne in a Red Armchair,* about 1877; Paul Cezanne, French [1839~1906]. Oil on canvas; unframed 72.5 x 56 cm [28 1/2 x 22 in.]. Bequest of Robertt Treat Paine 2nd, 44. 776), 87 above (*Houses at Auvers,* 1890; Vincent van Gogh, Dutch/ worked in France, [1853~1890]. Oil on canvas; unframed 75.5 x 61.8 cm [29 11/16 x 24 5/16 in.] . Bequest of John T. Spaulding, 48.549), 111 center (*Fruit Displayed on a Stand,* about 1880; Gustave Caillebotte, French [1848~1894]. Oil on canvas; unframed 76.5 x 100.5 cm [30 1/8 x 39 5/8 in.]. Fanny P. Mason Fund in Memory of Alice Thevin, 1979.196), and 120 below (*The Blue Boat,* 1892. Winslow Homer, American [1836~1910]. Watercolor over graphite on paper; Sheet 386 x 546 mm [15 3 /16 x 21 1/2 in.]. Bequest of William Sturgis Bigelow, 26.764), All works Courtesy Museum of Fine Arts, Boston. Reproduced with permission. © 1999 Museum of Fine Arts, Boston. All Rights Reserved; page 62 below is Courtesy **Gimpel Fils, London; English Heritage, London** for page 64 above (Photo: © English Heritage Photo Library); **Reunion des Musees Natiionaux** for pages 65 below (Musee Biot-Fernand Leger © RMN ~ ADAGP/Photo: © RMN~ Gerard Biot), 91 above (Musee des Antiquities Nationales/© Photo: RMN~J.G. Berizzi); **Wilton House, Salisbury,** UK for page 69 below (By Kind Permission of the Earl of Pembroke and the Trustees of Wilton House Trust, Wilton House); **The Wallace Collection, London** for page 75 (Reproduced by Kind Permission of the Trustees); **Hulton Getty Picture Collection, London** for page 77 above; **Brooklyn Museum of Art** for page 85 below; **The Collection of Andrew and Betsy Wyeth** © Andrew Wyeth for page 96; **The J. Paul Getty Museum, Los Angeles** for page 99 above; **Naturhistorisches Museum, Wien** for page 102 above right (Photo: Alice Schumacher); **Musee Rodin, Paris** for page 103 below right (Photo: Erik & Petra Hesmerg); **Chartres Cathedral, France** for page 107 below (Photo: Editions Hourvet); page 109 right is Reproduced by Kind Permission of **The National Trust for Scotland** (Photo:Martin Charles); **The William Morris Gallery, London, E.17** for page 117 above; page 118 is Reproduced by Permission of the Syndics of the **Fitzwilliam Museum, Cambridge; Elizabeth Blackadder OBE, RA** for page 120~121 above (Photo: © Royal Academy of Arts, London/Elizabeth Blackadder). The drawing on page 24 is from *The Gentle Art of Making* Enemies by J.A.M. Whistler, published 1892; the engravings on pages 42 below left and 124 above are from *The Complete Woodcuts of Albrecht Durer,* Edited by Dr. Willi Kurth. W & G Foyle Ltd 1927/Dover Publications, Inc 1963; the engraving on page 124 below is from *A General History of Quadrupeds,* by Thomas Bewick, first published in 1790 (Facsimile Edition published 1970 by Ward Lock Reprints).